MAIN LENDING   **<u>3 WEEK LOAN</u>**   DCU LIBRARY

Fines are charged **PER DAY** if this item is overdue.
Check at www.dcu.ie/~library or telephone (01) 700 5183 for fine rates and
renewal regulations for this item type.
Item is subject to recall.
Remember to use the Book Bin when the library is closed.
The item is due for return on or before the latest date shown below.

1 0 NOV 2007

For my late father, Matt, and my mother, Kitty:
it is because of their example of following Christ
according to their lights
that I continue to follow him according to mine.

Peadar Kirby

LESSONS IN LIBERATION

The Church in Latin America

Dominican Publications

First published 1981 by
Dominican Publications,
St Saviour's,
Dublin 1.

ISBN 0 907271 04 9

Cover design by Jarlath Hayes

Typesetting by Healyset, Dublin.

Printed in Ireland by Genprint, Dublin.

ACKNOWLEDGMENTS

The scripture quotations in this publication are from the Revised Standard Version of the Bible, copyrighted 1966 by the Division of Christian Education, of the National Council of the Churches of Christ in the USA. The Bible quotation in Chapter Three is from the *New English Bible.*

The author and publishers are grateful to the following for permission to use copyright material: to Sheed and Ward Ltd, for quotations from Helder Camara, *Spiral of Violence;* to Sheed and Ward Ltd and to Penguin Books Ltd for permission to quote from Paulo Freire, *Pedagogy of the Oppressed;* to Penguin Books Ltd for the quotation from John Gerassi (ed), *Camilo Torres: Revolutionary Priest;* to SCM Press for quotations from Gustavo Gutierrez, *A Theology of Liberation,* and from Jose P Miranda, *Marx and the Bible;* to SPCK for the quotation from Leonardo Boff, *Jesus Christ Liberator;* to Christian Journals Ltd for quotations from Mary Hall, *The Impossible Dream;* to the Irish Missionary Union for the quotation from *A New Missionary Era;* and to the National Conference of Catholic Bishops, Washington, for quotations from the *Puebla* documents.

CONTENTS

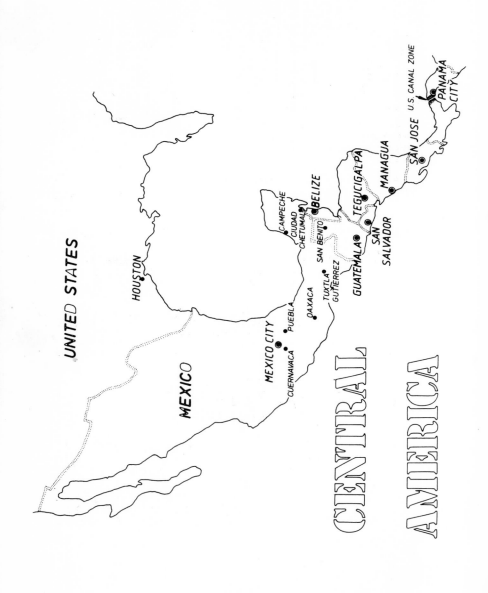

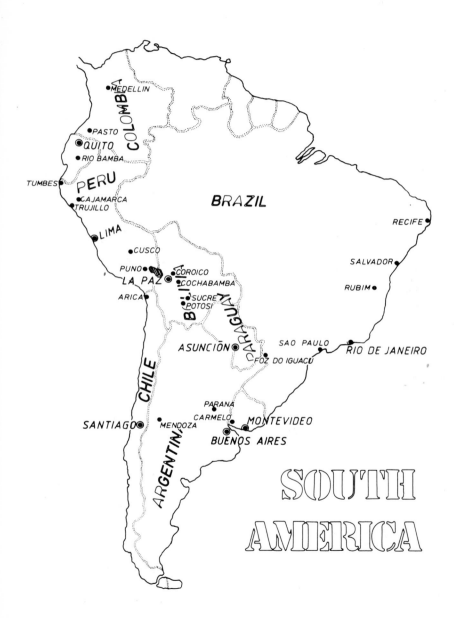

PREFACE

This book was born out of a discussion at Puebla with Gary McEoin, the well-known Irish American writer on church affairs, who has himself written on Latin America. I asked him simply whether it was foolish of someone who was going to spend just six to seven months travelling around the continent to think of writing a book on what is a very complex and varied subject. He answered that there are two occasions when someone can write the kind of book that was in my mind: on first impressions, and then only after a long acquaintance with the subject. My first impressions, he said, could be very valuable as a book. That was the decision to attempt this book.

But it is to my publisher, Fr Austin Flannery OP, that my main thanks must go. It is a much deeper debt I owe him than simply gratitude at suggesting that I write a book or agreeing to publish it; it is not too much to say that I wouldn't now be a professional writer without Austin's constant encouragement and even seeming pleasure at my first feeble attempts at articles. It was seeing these articles in print in *Doctrine and Life* that gave me the necessary affirmation to write more.

If it was Austin who made me feel I could write and had ideas worth writing about, it was another priest who, at an earlier phase in my life, gave me the support to continue my questioning and searching, Fr Frank Mullan CM, my superior in the Vincentians for three years. While Frank never fully agreed with all my conclusions, his breadth of mind and spirit always made me feel that what I was doing was important. The greatest tribute I can pay to Frank is that he will probably be surprised to read these words: What he did, he did totally naturally; there was nothing self-conscious about it.

This book just could not have been written without the astounding hospitality I received, particularly from Irish missionaries, all over Latin America. The list is far too long to mention everybody by name; but from Jaime Fogarty in Mexico City to Frank Murphy in Recife I received lodgings, companionship, insights and much help and contacts everywhere I went. Some of these people appear in the pages of the book, most do not; but this book results from all these people's concern to help me see and experience as much as I could of the Latin American reality.

If I single out the Columbans in Lima and Santiago, and the Holy

1

Ghost fathers and Holy Rosary sisters in Brazil, it is not because they did more for me than the others I met, but just because as groups they are easier to mention. Among all of these I encountered a realistic and down-to-earth commitment which it is not too strong to call an inspiration.

Finally, there are those friends at home who have supported me in various ways. My companions in the house I live in, Michael Rynne (who adapted the Portuguese text of the cartoons for use in the book) and his brother John, Chris Bluth, and Tim O'Neill, and especially Mike Kinneen, from whom one takes encouragement for granted, have put up with me. Tricia Coxon has been patient with my erratic writing, and has produced a neat and tidy typescript from my much-corrected copy. My good friend John MacNamara has drawn the maps of my travels.

At the end of the day, all that I have received from these people has been filtered through my perception of the world, my concern, my outlook. I am sure none of those who have helped me with this book will agree with everything in it. I hope none of them will find it inaccurate.

Peadar Kirby
Dublin
Ireland
22nd May 1980

INTRODUCTION

"I came that they may have life and have it more abundantly."
(John 10:10)

"You will know the truth and the truth will make you mad."
Sign in a sisters' house in Coroico, Bolivia.

This book is the result of a seven-month journey around Latin America in early 1979. That journey began in Mexico at the Third Conference of Latin American Bishops at the end of January, and ended in Recife in the Northeast of Brazil at the end of August.

I set out to visit many of the dioceses which had become well known for their advanced pastoral planning and activities and which were also the places to meet the most advanced bishops and theologians. In each place I visited I tried to meet the bishop and other leaders, whether theologians or pastoral workers, lay and clerical. But I also went out of my way to spend time around the shanty towns talking to the people and sitting in on their meetings and liturgies.

My route took me down through Mexico and into Belize. From there I crossed into the north of Guatemala and joined the Panamerican highway at Guatemala City. That took me down through the capitals of El Salvador, Honduras, Nicaragua and Costa Rica to Panama City. There the road ended and I had to fly to Medellin in Colombia. I then went by road down through Colombia to Quito, the capital of Ecuador, and after that to the city of Riobamba, five hours south of Quito, the most progressive diocese in both those countries.

From Ecuador I headed south into Peru and spent Easter in the town of Cajamarca in the Andes, the town where Pizarro captured the Emperor of the Incas in November 1532. Coming back down to the coast I spent Easter week in Trujillo, Peru's second city and then went down to Lima. From there I broke all my records with a fiftyone-hour bus ride to Cusco at eleven thousand feet above sea level, the capital of the Inca empire and the centre for visiting the magnificent ruins of their highly developed culture.

I continued along the *altiplano* at twelve thousand feet to Puno on Lake Titicaca and from there to the Bolivian capital, La Paz. This was my centre for a tour northwards to Coroico at the edge of the great expanse of jungle that stretches up into Brazil, a town reached along one of the most spectacular roads in the world cut out of rock into the edge of the sheer face of the mountain. I also went south to the mining city of Potosi and back through Sucre, the legal capital of Bolivia, and Cochabamba to La Paz.

I then took the only means of transport available, a train that would be an antique at home, across the Andes down to Arica at the edge of the desert in the north of Chile and from there down through the Atacama desert to Santiago. From Santiago I crossed the Andes for the last time through the two kilometre-long international tunnel where our bus had to wait until the train in the tunnel had come through, since there is only room for one or the other at the same time.

That brought me into Argentina to the city of Mendoza and from there across the rich pampas to Buenos Aires. I crossed the estuary of the River Plate for Montevideo in Uruguay, and from there headed back into Argentina to Parana. That put me on the road to Asuncion, the capital of Paraguay.

From Asuncion I crossed my last international frontier into Brazil where, situated at the meeting of the borders of Argentina, Paraguay and Brazil, is what must be one of the world's most spectacular sights, the Iguacu waterfalls. I went from there to the continent's largest and fastest-growing city, Sao Paulo, the showpiece of Brazil's economic development and also the centre of its labour agitation.

Next came Rio de Janeiro, a marked contrast to the ugliness of Sao Paulo in a setting that must be, without doubt, the most magnificent of any city in the world. From Rio I visted a rural parish, Rubim, and continued northwards through Salvador, one of the country's first cities, on to Recife, the city of Latin America's most famous bishop, Dom Helder Camara.

I travelled always by bus; and where there was a choice between a luxury service and a second class one, I usually chose the latter. This enabled me to meet and chat to the local people though it also meant some adventures like getting left behind on the Guatemala-El Salvador border because I was the only passenger who had to get my passport stamped, or having the bus break down four hours outside La Paz at twelve thousand feet and feeling the bitter cold when the sun went down.

While this book is not a travelogue (there are plenty of those available), it is a book of impressions: an attempt to give the flavour of the consciousness and activities of Latin American Christians. Everything here is a result of what I saw and the people I met, and I include in this description my translations of some of the many documents — pastoral letters, pastoral plans, educational booklets, information booklets — that I picked up en route.

As such, this is not an analysis of the Latin American Church. Some readers will undoubtedly find it very subjective and uncritical, but this is a measure of how impressed and excited I was by what I saw and heard. Neither is this a balanced account: though I speak of the church in Latin America, that does not imply that all Latin American Christians think and act in the way I portray. My defence for this is simple: what

I present is not just a movement within the church. A whole new way of living as church is being born. That is what is important and significant about the Latin American Church; and so that is what I present in as comprehensive and accurate a way as I can. I can see no value in describing a church that acts in more or less the same way as does the church at home.

Another explanation is necessary. Any reader will quickly realise that I almost never mention Catholic or Protestant and, in fact, deal virtually exclusively with Catholics and Catholic situations. The main reason for this is that the distinction between Catholic and Protestant is not a significant difference any more for those Christians who understand and live out their faith in the new ways described in this book. If I intruded with such distinctions, I would be intruding a consciousness that belongs to the church in the developed world and would be falsifying the consciousness of Latin American Christians. That the situations I deal with are almost exclusively Catholic is more the accident of my contacts and my background, as well, of course, as being because the vast majority of Latin American Christians are Catholic. But it is important to remember that what is happening in the Catholic Church is happening in exactly the same way within the mainstream Protestant Churches.

This book then is a committed work rather than a dispassionate work. I would find it hard to conceive of a simple description of the Latin American Church that did not take sides: it provokes people, as Jesus did, to be for or against. I make no apologies in being for, and in saying that I believe this to be the only understanding of the Gospel and the only way of being church that makes sense today and is faithful and obedient to the message of Jesus.

The structure of this book itself expresses this new self-understanding of the Latin American Church. The first chapter sets the historical and social context of poverty and repression since it is the church's efforts to respond in a meaningful way to this situation that has motivated and conditioned all the change that has taken place. Chapter two is about the most important and significant response to these social conditions, namely the basic communities of the poor and oppressed themselves.

Chapter three goes into the overriding educational commitment of the Latin American Church making the oppressed aware of their oppression and its concrete causes by the economic and political system, what the Latin Americans call conscientisation. Chapter four shows how the wider organisations of the church — parishes, dioceses, and other specially constituted organisations — have made the liberation of the oppressed their overriding concern. Chapter five outlines the history and content of the theology of liberation, which seeks to articulate this new understanding the poor and oppressed have of their faith.

Chapter six gives three examples of how missionaries in different parts of the continent serve this popular church. Chapter seven takes examples of bishops who have committed themselves to the liberation of the oppressed. Chapter eight outlines the background tensions and the day by day events of the Puebla conference and evaluates its controversial conclusions. Chapter nine gives some Latin American views of the church in the developed world of Europe and North America, and draws the lessons for us.

In its structure then, this book makes the point that the overriding concern of the Latin American Church is the liberation of the oppressed and shows how this is not something imposed from above but rather something that has grown from the grass-roots of the church, from the poor and oppressed themselves. The other levels of the church have then re-organised themselves to make this liberation their central aim.

Each chapter begins with a short introduction to the topic and gives three or four different and varied examples of the topic in action. Each section stands independently on its own but they all serve to compliment one another. I make much use of quotations, whether it is interviews with bishops or theologians, translations of documents or just the comments I noted down from the many people I met. Some readers may find the use of quotes excessive. If stylistically this is so, I decided on it because I hope it will give a more immediate flavour of the consciousness of people at all levels of the church.

For the same reason I include illustrations from booklets published in Latin America, translating the captions into English. These graphic examples of the catechetical work of the Latin American church all come from Brazil. Most are taken from a simplified version of the Puebla documents, *Puebla Para o Povo.* The remainder come from a catechetical programme, *O Reino de Deus esta entre Nos,* and a popular edition of a pastoral letter of the Brazilian bishops, *Exigencias Cristas de una Ordem Politica.*

Finally I would like to borrow some words of Archbishop Helder Camara to express my aim in writing this book: "Leave no one indifferent around you. Provoke discussions. Your youth must force people to think and take up a position: let it be uncomfortable like truth, demanding like justice."[1] If this book does not provoke, then it has failed.

Chapter One

THE CONTEXT:
HISTORICAL AND SOCIAL SITUATION

"The Lord enters into judgment with the elders and princes of his people: 'It is you who have devoured the vineyard, the spoil of the poor is in your houses. What do you mean crushing my people, by grinding the face of the poor?', says the Lord God of hosts."
Isaiah, 3:14-15

"The blatant and striking contrast between those who possess nothing and those who show off their opulence is an insuperable obstacle in establishing the reign of peace."
Puebla, 138

One cannot begin to understand the Latin American Church until one understands its context, because the enormous changes that have taken place in that church over the past ten to fifteen years have not come from episcopal plans but rather from the efforts of individuals and groups at all levels of the church, and notably at the grass-roots, to face up seriously to that context.

In the continent with the largest number of Catholics in the world, the church has always been an important influence in Latin American society. And that society has always been characterised by poverty and exploitation of a most naked and brutal kind. Neither have there been lacking individuals and groups who felt such poverty and exploitation to be an affront to their Christian conscience and who energetically denounced it, some to the point of taking up arms to change it.

What has changed is that for the first time ever in Latin America, and indeed in almost any part of the world, the church as church as distinct from small groups within it, has begun to do this. Whole dioceses have re-organised themselves in such a way that the liberation of the oppressed becomes their overriding pastoral priority. Episcopal conferences have spoken out in the most forceful way, denouncing the model of society and of the economy operating in their countries. Theological debate has come to be dominated by the needs of the oppressed.

The Latin American church therefore cannot be understood apart

8

from that context. The aim of this chapter is to fill in that context. First, there is a brief history of the church in that continent, highlighting particularly the dissident strands that have always been there. The second part gives three examples of the appalling social conditions in which most Latin Americans lives. Part three outlines some of the statistics of repression which are a fact of life in almost every country of the continent; and part four gives a brief description of the model of society operating there seen through the eyes of the Brazilian episcopal conference.

A History of Contradiction

Latin America was not discovered in 1492; that year marks rather the beginning of its integration into a European, and more recently North American, economy and culture. In this historical process the church has been, at one and the same time, both the vehicle of this integration and the prophetic voice speaking out against it.

The mass conversions of the Indian peoples, especially those advanced cultures of the Aztecs and Mayans in Mexico and the Incas in Peru, went side by side with a deliberate and brutal effort to wipe out their achievements. While the Spanish Crown was melting down the beautiful gold and silver work to stave off bankruptcy, the church was obliterating the native learning.

Of the extensive collections of Mayan books the conquerers found, only three books were saved from the zeal of Bishop Diego de Landa who boasted that he had "burned them all" because "they contained nothing in which there was not to be seen superstitition and lies of the devil."[1] Not only were whole cultures obliterated but it is estimated that some fifty million Indians died in those early decades of conquest.

But alongside the destructive zeal of the missionaries was the enlightened preaching in defence of the rights of the Indians particularly of the Dominican Bartolome de las Casas who petitioned the King of Spain again and again to protect the Indians from the virtual slavery they were being reduced to. Even in that first century of colonisation churchmen were martyred for their defence of the Indians, among them the bishop of Nicaragua, Antonio Valdivieso.

It is for this reason therefore that Jose Comblin has written: "From the beginning, evangelisation was a contradiction in Latin America, because...the Church was divided between one part which was the church of the 'conquistadores' and another part which accepted responsibility for defending the human and social rights of the indigenous people."[2]

As the church established itself as an organ of the Spanish and Portuguese Crowns in Latin America, so too did sectors continue their

defence of the oppressed. Most notable among these were the Jesuits who set up self-governing communities of Guarani Indians in the area where the borders of present-day Paraguay, Brazil and Argentina meet.

· Beginning in the middle of the seventeenth century, some one hundred thousand Indians eventually lived in more than thirty of these *communes* whose ideals could be described as socialist inspired. The products of the community's work were distributed to each according to need; and the old, the sick and others who could not work were supported by the community. The Indians were taught skills, some even learning to print books in their own language, Guarani, which the Jesuits systematised and put in written form for the first time. The Jesuits finally handed over control of the communities to elected councils of the Indians.

These communities ended abruptly in 1768 when the Spanish king, under pressure from whites greedy for land and more Indians to work it for them, decreed the destruction of the communities and the expulsion of the Jesuits. The Indians were at the mercy of the whites; and the Jesuits were sent home in chains.

As well as running these communities, Jesuits were writing extensively about the New World, dispelling many of the myths which the colonisers had built up about the inferior nature of the native peoples of Latin America. As such they are considered the literary precursors of American nationalism.

The first thirty years of the nineteenth century saw struggles for independence all over the continent, led by a local middle class strongly influenced by the ideals of the French Revolution. Here again the contradictions of the Latin American church are to be seen: The bishops and higher clergy, who depended on the Spanish and Portuguese Crowns for their patronage, totally opposed the independence movements; but some of these movements were led by priests.

The notable example of this is in Mexico where independence was gained through the guerrilla struggles led by Miguel Hidalgo, a priest, who organised the Indians in a violent social protest. When he was captured and executed, his place was taken by another priest, Jose Maria Morelos, who managed to widen the social support for the revolution and beat the Spanish forces in a brilliant military campaign.

In Brazil, it was a priest, Diogo Antonio Feijo, who became the first regent of the new state in 1835-37 and who led the anti-clerical forces in establishing the primacy of the civil over the ecclesiastical authority and who confiscated the wealth of the religious orders.

These notable examples proved the exception, however; and the church, by and large, never accommodated itself to the newly independent states. Because of this, it cemented an alliance with the landed oligarchy, who had also been opposed to independence; and it lost the support of the liberal middle class who took control after independence. The church, however, did keep the support of the oppressed masses; and church activity came to depend more on a devotional and conservative brand of religion, the effect of which was to keep the poor subservient. It also began to rely more and more on its links with Rome to strengthen its position. Archbishop McGrath of Panama City sums up the church at the end of the nineteenth century as being "a very tired church, a very divided church, a very weakened church."

Not until the 1930's did the official church finally began to accommodate itself to the status quo. The pressure came from the new phase of development the continent was entering with populist dictators, inspired by the examples of fascism in Europe, coming to power under the banner of uniting the nation. Following vigorous policies of industrialisation, dictators like Vargas in Brazil (1930–45 and 1950–54), Peron in Argentina (1945-55) and to a lesser extent President Cardenas in Mexico (1934-40) looked to the church to deliver the masses to support their populist policies. This was also in the interests of the church at the time, as church leaders were becoming worried by the inroads of Marxism in the new urban proletariat.

The church fell in fully behind this new drive and, borrowing models from Europe, helped to set up Christian trade unions and Christian Democratic Parties in many states. The model of a new Christian civilisation under the leadership of a strong but benign father-figure was evolved and was often called 'the new Christendom'.

Only in the sixties did this model finally break down. The pressures of the international market, and particularly the need for new technology to compete with the products of the developed world, led to the increasing penetration of foreign capital, most notably in the form of multinational companies. With the crisis of native capitalism the local bourgeoisie saw their interest more and more as being with that foreign capital; and to this end the populist effort to buy the support of the urban proletariat was finally sacrificed.

The increasing inroads of the multi-nationals in the sixties saw, therefore, a growing impoverishment of the masses, and led directly to the breakdown of the democratic systems of almost all the Latin American states, a process begun by the take-over by the military in Brazil in 1964. Military take-overs were the signal for the unleashing of a whole system of repression to stamp out the discontent of the masses. As one Latin American theologian, Pablo Richard, sums up this process: "Only those sectors of the bourgeoisie tied to big multinational capital enriched themselves. All the rest − the medium and small industrialists, and especially the lower classes, − entered into an accelerated process of pauperisation."[3]

As a response to this, and given impetus by the victory of the Cuban revolutionaries in 1959, a strong revolutionary ferment was growing. This had a big influence on sectors of the church, notably among the working class and students; and resulted either in many leaving the church, or in setting up a dualism whereby conservative religious ideas and practice went hand in hand with revolutionary political ideas and practice. Meanwhile, many among the more aware in the leadership of the church were forced to question the openly repressive policies of the state, and they moved painfully into a phase of criticism of the excesses of state power.

The decade from the mid-sixties to the mid-seventies witnessed greater and more significant changes in the Latin American church than had taken place in the whole four hundred and fifty years up to then. This period began with the symbolic example of Camilo Torres killed in the mountains of Colombia in 1966 after he decided to live out his priesthood among the guerrillas of Colombia, a lone witness to a new understanding of Christianity.

In that decade one man's lone understanding became a broad and challenging movement within the Church. Already in 1966 basic Christian communities were beginning in Chile and Brazil, small groups of

Christians supporting one another in discovering a new meaning to their faith in the midst of the struggles of the oppressed. This new meaning was reflected upon and articulated by a group of young theologians and sympathetic bishops, and found public and authoritative expression in some of the conclusions of the second Conference of Latin American Bishops at Medellin in 1968.

With the growth of repressive dictatorships and their clamp down on trade unions and political parties, these church groups increasingly became the only forum where people could share their fears and hopes. The movement towards basic communities spread rapidly in the years after Medellin as much for this reason as for the encouragement given them by the bishops.

The victory of Salvador Allende in Chile in 1970 proved yet another factor in convincing many Christians of the possibility of radical social change. The efforts being made by the Allende government to allow the people far more power over their own affairs as well as to distribute income and resources far more equally contrasted strongly with the policies being followed in most other countries which were resulting in a greater concentration of wealth and power in fewer and fewer hands. That the latter governments all called themselves christian was seen more and more by leading churchmen as a direct insult to the church.

The founding of Christians for Socialism in Santiago in 1972 served to shock many church leaders into a realisation of just how much their traditional theology supported in effect an unjust system under the guise of being disinterested in politics. It also marked the coming of age of a new integration between Christian faith and political commitment, an end to the dualism under which religious and political beliefs were seen as separate entities.

The savage overthrow of Salvador Allende led to a new stage of maturity and realism on the part of many Christians. No longer could

the difficulties be underestimated; and with the increasing repression and impoverishment of the majority, sectors of the church became more and more clear that their option was with that oppressed majority. This book is about that option.

The Faces of Poverty

"The vast majority of our fellow humans continue to live in a situation of poverty and even wretchedness that has grown more acute." *(Puebla, par. 1135)* Thus did the bishops of Latin America baldly characterise what is the single most important fact of life in that continent today. But as much as I had read about it or seen films of it, the reality of the conditions in which the majority live in Latin America was indeed an acute shock when I could actually touch and smell and feel it. And you can never get away from it because wherever you go it is there: enormous shanty towns encircling every city and town, clusters of tiny mud huts in the countryside. The following are three typical examples.

Miguel is twenty-eight. He lives in the western highlands of Guatemala with Maria his wife and his five young children, and owns a plot which is roughly one tenth of an acre. He is typical of 75% of the country's population, whose tiny plots occupy just 19% of the country's arable land. Guatemala's best land, along the Pacific coast, grows rich coffee and banana crops; but is owned by a mere 2% of the population though it accounts for 63% of the arable land.

Every November Miguel and his family join 1½ million other campesinos (peasants) who travel in lorries down to these plantations in an effort to earn enough money in the three month harvest season to tide them over for the rest of the year. Here they work a ten to twelve hour day in the hot sun picking the ripe coffee berries into huge baskets. Paid by the basket, the average they earn is 75p to £1 a day.

The families are provided with accommodation on the plantations: huge open shelters with just a tin or straw roof over them. Here they sleep with up to fifty other families on the mud floor in their working clothes. There is no clean water, no toilet facilities. A small meal is provided three times a day. But it is only given to the men who are working, so Miguel has to share his six small tortillas (a type of pancake made from cornmeal) and one ounce of black beans with his wife and children.

Come February, the families migrate back to their poor land in the highlands, lucky if some of the family have not caught one of many diseases from the lack of hygiene, the hunger, or the wet nights under the open shelter. As often as not some of the hard earned money will be owed for loans made to tide Miguel and his family over the nine lean months of the year. The cycle will begin again the following November.

Juan is twenty six. He lives in the city of Potosi at an altitude of 12,000 feet in the Andes of southern Bolivia. He is a miner, of Indian stock, and has been working for ten years in the privately owned tin mines on the Cerro Rico overlooking the city. This rich mountain first lured the Spaniards to this part of the continent in 1545 when they discovered the deposits of silver it contained. In the next hundred years Potosi became one of the world's biggest and richest cities equal in population to the city of London at the time.

But it also became the terror of the Indians as far away as Peru, who were recruited to work in slavery to satisfy the greed of the Spaniards. By the end of the seventeenth century the silver was exhausted and Potosi settled into decline.

Juan mines the Cerro for tin together with about six thousand others. Though this tin earns Bolivia three quarters of its foreign income the miners see little of this money. Average incomes at about £150 per head per annum, are the second lowest in Latin America. Juan can earn around 75p a day in the privately owned mines where two thirds of the miners of Potosi work. The main difference between his conditions and those of the more privileged miners in the state-owned mines is not in their daily income, these are roughly the same. The difference lies rather in the working conditions.

Juan works just as his ancestors did under the Spaniards three hundred years ago, with no protective clothing or modern equipment of any kind, working in mine shafts that date back hundreds of years and still have some small buildings at their entrances dating from Spanish times. He showed me the shrines to the devil, with their daily offerings, inside each mine shaft. These shrines take pride of place over those to the Virgin Mary. The state mines, however, have modern equipment and the miners are given periodic medical checks. They are also given tiny shacks to live in for as long as they work (though they can be evicted at any time as has happened to miners active in trade union work) and they get meagre pensions when they retire.

The average working life of Juan and his colleagues in fifteen years, and their average life expectancy is thirty-five years due to silicosis, a disease of the lungs. Juan expects to be able to work for just another five years. He does not know what he will do then.

Joao is thirty six. He lives in the Baixada Fluminense on the outskirts of Rio de Janeiro, known as the city's 'dormitory' because 70% of its population sleep there. Joao gets up at 4.00 every morning to join the million and half other workers commuting the twenty-five miles across the city to work. He has to walk two miles to the bus terminal because that is his only hope of getting on one of the packed buses. Here he joins a long queue to wait his turn.

Buses are so packed that people have to fight their way in. At times they hang on to the outside of the doors in order to get to work on time. Once on the bus it is often impossible to push one's way through the tightly packed crowd to get off. The suburban trains are worse, with people regularly killed when they lose their foothold by the door. If Joao arrives five minutes late for his work he automatically loses his day's pay; if he arrives late three different days, he is sacked. Starting at 7.00, he works through to 5.00, and begins the same battle to get home, where he arrives at around 7.30 to 8.00 p.m.

For this he earns the average minimum wage in Brazil, which is £30 a month. It has been calculated that this will buy for himself, his wife and four children, a small cup of concentrated coffee and one bun four times a day for the month. Almost half of Brazil's workers have to live on this, and enormous numbers remain unemployed. Though the cost of living has risen 850% since 1972, the basic minimum wage is, in real terms, less than half of what it was twenty years ago.

The much praised 'economic miracle' of Brazil, the 10% per annum growth of her economy between 1968 and 1973, has in effect made the rich richer and the poor poorer. In 1960 5% of the population received 28% of the national income: their share has now risen to 39%. For half the population, their share of the national 'cake' fell from 18% in 1960 to 12% in 1978. The real 'economic miracle' of Brazil is how Joao, and millions like him, live at all.

The Institutions of Violence

The tragic murder of Archbishop Romero of San Salvador on the night of Monday, 24th March, 1980, as he said Mass in the cancer hospital where he lived, drew the attention of the world to the courageous role some Latin American bishops have taken up as spokesmen for the poor and oppressed. But it takes the murder of a bishop to draw attention to what has become a way of life in many Latin American countries, as repressive oligarchies try to contain the cries of protest of the majority at a situation of increasing impoverishment.

In the archdiocese of San Salvador alone, six priests have been murdered by the military over the past three years. All over the continent it is estimated that the number of priests killed, tortured or expelled, because of their option for the poor, is now over nine hundred. And if there are over nine hundred priests, how many thousands of other committed people have suffered the same fate?

Amnesty International maintains the most comprehensive and systematic monitoring of the abuses of human rights. The survey of Latin America in their 1979 annual report makes chilling reading. Apart from the small countries of Belize, Honduras, Costa Rica, Panama and the Guyanas, they find every country of mainland Latin America guilty of "arbitrary arrests, torture, politically motivated disappearances, long-term detention without charge or trial, extrajudicial executions, political murders and the death penalty."[4] Even worse, they go on to say that "in many countries, these violations of basic human rights are facilitated by emergency legislation which is used mainly to legalise political repression and to perpetuate authoritarian regimes."

Amnesty have a list of over two thousand five hundred people missing in Argentina, all arrested by the police, but whose existence or whereabouts are denied by the government. However, some of their bodies have been found, all with bullet wounds. Twelve such bodies were washed ashore at a seaside resort in December 1978 amid fears that many more of the disappeared may have been killed.

In Chile too more than fifteen hundred people of the political parties which supported Salvador Allende disappeared between 1973 and 1977. Again, bodies of some of these have been found, and the government continues to refuse to allow an independent enquiry into the whereabouts of the majority of the disappeared. Moreover, Amnesty reports that they are concerned by reports that "great numbers of arbitrary arrests, short-term disappearances and cases of torture continue". They add that "ill-treatment and torture usually take place before the detained person is brought before the courts."

Amnesty has documented cases of torture in Brazil despite government assurances that it had ended. Sixty people arrested or abducted between 1969 and 1975 remain unaccounted for, and recent reports indicate that Brazilian police are arresting Argentinians, Uruguayans and Chileans wanted for political reasons at home, and secretely handing them over to the police forces of their own countries.

Colombia has been under a state of siege since 1948, a situation made worse by the enactment of a new Security Act in 1978 inhibiting the right of defence of political detainees, eliminating the right to appeal, and widening the scope of military tribunals. Despite the President's insistence that "absolutely no one in Colombia has been tortured", Amnesty reports that about fifty methods of torture, ranging from psychological methods to the use of drugs and electric shocks, continue to be used in a widespread way.

In El Salvador "the repression continued and violence got worse," Amnesty says. The scale of torture and disappearances is now so great that Fr Sobrino recently described it as "genocide". Mutilated bodies are found daily and one local human rights organisation put the number of those murdered, often after horrible torture, as being two thousand three hundred in the first six months of 1980.

Amnesty has reported more than twenty thousand politically motivated murders or disappearances in Guatemala since 1966. In 1979, it said, these "continued to be endemic. Political murder and torture, sometimes at the hands of the official security forces, sometimes following abduction by paramilitary death squads, are widespread. Identification of the victims is often difficult because their bodies are mutilitated and found far from the original place of abduction."

In Paraguay, though the state of siege which has been in force for the twenty five years of General Stroessner's rule applies now only to the capital city, Asuncion, Amnesty is concerned that "longstanding serious human rights problems remain." People continue to be detained without trial, and tortured; some died in 1979 as a result of the use of torture.

The Peruvian authorities, according to Amnesty, make periodic large-scale, short-term arrests of trade unionists, political activists and community leaders who work in the shanty towns surrounding the main cities. Military courts have had their powers extended, and civilians are now brought before them as a matter of routine. Cases of torture also continue to be documented by Amnesty in Peru.

Uruguay, Amnesty finds guilty of a "persistent pattern of gross violations of human rights" and notes that two thousand five hundred to two thousand eight hundred political prisoners continue to be held (1 per 1,000 inhabitants) which doesn't include those arrested, interrogated, tortured and released without being brought before a court.

Torture and arrest of civilians by the military continues in Venezuala with one hundred and eighty civilian prisoners held under military justice in 1979.

Violation of the basic rights of large numbers of people all over Latin America then is not some passing aberration of justice, but is rather a necessary system to maintain the ruling oligarchies in power. As Archbishop Romero stated in an interview just two weeks before he was killed: "The repression against the people is transformed into a necessity in order to maintain and increase the profit margins, even at the cost of the increasing poverty of the working class."[5]

The need to justify this systematic repression has given rise to a doctrine called the Ideology of National Security. Since Brazil was the first country to build up a system of repression in the sixties, it was Brazilian strategists who first elaborated the doctrine. It sees the world divided between two warring power blocs, Communism and what is called 'Western Christian civilisation.' From such a standpoint any protest is easily seen as 'Communist subversion' and thus the military feel justified in using any means necessary to stamp it out, including the centralisation of power in their own hands. The doctrine was condemned at Puebla as not being 'compatible with the Christian vision of the human being' (par 549).

A Slave Society

Church leaders have not been content just to condemn this situation of growing poverty and repression; neither has their response remained on the level of giving hand-outs to the people. They have sought rather to analyse and get down to the root causes of the situation. As the Puebla documents say: "Analysing this situation more deeply, we discover that this poverty is not a passing phase. Instead it is the product of economic, social and political situations and structures . . . [which] create a situation on the international level where the rich get richer at the expense of the poor who get ever poorer."

The Brazilian conference of bishops has been one of the more systematic in conducting such an analysis. In August 1979 they published a forceful document entitled 'Points for a Social Policy' which rigorously uncovers the model of society which exists in Brazil today.

"In the way the Brazilian political and economic model has functioned

historically, no matter how much at times it has resulted in economic growth, it has always been based on structural injustice," the bishops begin. They then go on to describe more fully how this operates today.

They document in detail the concentration of wealth in fewer and fewer hands, a process which has grown so much greater in the last twenty years. "We are dealing with a situation of injustice which has assumed such proportions as are not even found in the most advanced capitalist economies," they say. They go on: "Brazilian society today, in terms of the basic elements of its structure, has not come far from the slave society in which it originated. Using the symbols of a slave society, we can say that there exist on the one hand the masters of the means of production, surrounded by a constellation of technocratic majordomos; on the other hand are the great anonymous majority at the service of these masters. The masters have access to consuming all the goods they want from the most simple to the most scandalous. The servants survive, that is to say they have access to the goods and services necessary to guarantee their survival and reproduction without which the system would be condemned to collapse.

"It is difficult to eliminate the painful impression that the shape of the economy, the school system, the administration of justice, the system of credit, the organisation of the city and its relations with the countryside were planned by the masters to guarantee first and foremost their own interests. In the name of these interests the people produce thousands of cars which they will never drive; they build thousands of apartments which they will never live in; and they construct sophisticated airports which they will never use."

The document then takes up specific issues responsible for perpetuating this model of society. The multinational companies have "reduced our national autonomy and made our economy more dependent on the developed economies of the world." The multinationals favour "the concentration of wealth, speculation . . . investment in ostentatious goods at the expense of the increase of the national debt and . . . have grave consequences for the acceleration of inflation."

The bishops go on to question the government's way of fighting inflation by raising the salaries of those already well off in order to increase incentives for productive industry instead of concentrating on efforts to use productively the huge potential of the unemployed.

The consequences of such an economic model are that "our greatest resource, our people, is not valued." Here they list four groups, the marginalised, the unemployed, the wastefully employed and the underemployed. "The change in our social and political system must invest in the person," they conclude, "creating conditions which give value to the person. This must be the decisive criterion for change, and it is not alone necessary but urgent."

The final third of the document is entitled: "What is hoped from a new system." The first hope is for a revision in wages tied to the rise in the cost of living. There must be an "effective share in profits and the increases in productivity, and progressive correction in the distortions in incomes which have got so bad recently."

The second hope is for "rigorously and unalterably frozen prices of basic goods linked to heavy taxation of sophisticated consumption." There must be means to "stimulate investment for collective and social uses and disincentives for investment in superfluous and conspicuous consumption."

There is a need to "urgently improve the shanty towns, giving them the services guaranteed to the rest of the population" and linked to this "statutes to control the use and possession of urban land." Furthermore, the government must "allow the creation of real mechanisms by which the people can participate in power" including "genuine freedom and autonomous trade unions" and they must "recognise and accept the means of participation which the people are creating."

The bishops end by saying that they are "transmitting the ideas, aspirations and criticisms of the grass-roots." "If we didn't speak of these problem which afflict our people, the exercise of other aspects of our mission would lose credibility and persuasive force," they say, "and would merit the biblical condemnation of false prophets."

The situation described by the Brazilian bishops can be generalised for the continent as a whole. They speak out not because they hope that by speaking they will change the situation. Rather they see themselves as the mouthpiece for those who alone can really change it: the poor and oppressed who daily suffer under the present system. These people are the basic priority for the Latin American Church and therefore they are the starting point for this book.

Chapter Two

BASIC COMMUNITIES:
THE PEOPLE'S CHURCH

"Has not God chosen those who are poor in the world to be rich in faith and heirs of the kingdom which he has promised to those who love him? But you have dishonoured the poor man. Is it not the rich who oppress you, is it not they who drag you into court?"
James, 2:5-6

"The common enemy of us all, this dependent capitalist system, is like the dragon of the Apocalypse. The small and fragile communities are like the woman who groans with the pains of childbirth in order to bring forth the new life that conquers the dragon."
LETTER TO CHRISTIANS WHO LIVE AND CELEBRATE THEIR FAITH IN POPULAR CHRISTIAN COMMUNITIES IN THE POOR COUNTRIES OF THE THIRD WORLD
issued after the Fourth International Conference of the Ecumenical Association of Third World Theologians in Sao Paulo, March 1980

The most important development in the Latin American Church in recent time has been the growth of *communidades de base,* or basic communities (CEBs).* Puebla singled them out when it said: "Over the past ten years they have multiplied and matured, particularly in some countries, so that now they are one of the causes for joy and hope in the church . . . centres of evangelization and moving forces for liberation and development". (par 96). Their unique importance was further underlined by the Seventh General Assembly of Latin American

---

*For anyone writing on basic communities in English a problem of translation arises. There does not seem yet to be any accepted translation for the term *Communidad de Base*. While 'grassroots community' would be the most accurate English translation, I opt for the term 'basic community' as it is closer to the Spanish term and also serves to show that they are not just one more new type of community alongside those already existing in the church, but are in fact a new model for the church itself. For simple convenience, I will use the Spanish abbreviation based on the three initial letters in the term *communidad eclesial de base*, CEB, which is the term normally used in Latin America when speaking or writing about basic communities.

Religious in March 1979 when it called them "the most significant pastoral response of our church".

Basic communities are not simply a new movement within the church. They are a new type of basic cell structure of the church, the first time in centuries that any significant sector of the church has developed new grass-roots structures for living out the faith. As such they constitute a whole new view of what being church involves, with enormous implications for every other level of the church from parishes, local clergy and theologians to dioceses, bishops, episcopal conferences and right up to CELAM, the Conference of Latin American Bishops. The first part of this chapter draws out these implications.

To illustrate different aspects of the life of a basic Christian community, I then take examples of how they operate in four places I visited: Cuernavaca in Mexico, San Salvador the capital of El Salvador, Panama City, and Santiago, Chile. In Cuernavaca basic communities were developed as early as the mid sixties so they serve to show different phases of growth they can go through. The San Salvador and Panama examples show in different ways how they relate to the parish structure. The two Santiago examples show both the complex organisational structure of a CEB and something of the support and friendship they provide. All these examples together serve to illustrate the differences in how CEBs live their lives in practice because they grow up as living communities responding to people's needs not being imposed from above according to an already worked-out blueprint. Yet they all do conform to a radically new view of being church.

What are CEBs?

The most concise description of what CEBs are comes from paragraphs 641 and 642 of the Puebla documents:

As a community, the CEB brings together families, adults and young people, in an intimate interpersonal relationship grounded in the faith. As an ecclesial reality, it is a community of faith, hope and charity. It celebrates the Word of God and takes its nourishment from the Eucharist, the culmination of all the sacraments. It fleshes out the Word of God in life through solidarity and commitment to the new commandment of the Lord; and through the service of approved co-ordinators, it makes present and operative the mission of the church and its visible communion with the legitimate pastors. It is a base-level body because it is composed of relatively few members as a permanent body, like a cell of the larger community. "When they deserve their ecclesial designation, they can take charge of their own spiritual and human existence in a spirit of fraternal solidarity." (Paul VI)

United in a CEB and nurturing their adherence to Christ, Christians strive for a more evangelical way of life amid the people, work together to challenge the egotistical and consumeristic roots of society, and make explicit their vocation to communion with God and their fellow humans. Thus they offer a valid and worthwhile departure for building up a new society, the civilisation of love.

It was Archbishop McGrath of Panama City, a diocese in which basic communities have been well developed, who fleshed out the rather formal language of the Puebla description for me, showing how basic communities are developed in practice:

It is the pastor who realises that his community is large and fractured and scattered, and to try to bring them all together is an impossible task. So he goes at them in community fashion. First of all, he tries to bring out of each group a few persons who can be converted to the Word and to a spiritual and sacramental life with a sense of the Gospel and evangelisation. Then, he trains them to go into the group to be evangelizers, the basic team for that group: it may be a couple, it may be two or three men. The priest, of course, doesn't abandon those areas, he goes there; but he'll be working mainly through his team with whom he'll have periodic retreats and days of study and recollection. But they themselves are charged with the knowledge of the Word, the commitment to the Christian life, the Christian Way, and then the sacramental preparation, and in some cases, also part of the sacramental life, baptism, bringing communion to the sick and so forth. So it is an organic thing and it works from life. It is somewhat like the old cell idea of specialised Catholic Action but in a much fuller sense. The cell only existed for penetration of the body. In this sense, it was an elite to work upon the mass. But this is church, this group is considered to be the full living of the church but then to be shared in a fuller communion with the church.

The CEB is therefore a small group of committed Christians. Their unity is not based on a specialised interest, as is the case in the various movements such as the Saint Vincent de Paul Society or Christian Family Movement, which we know. They are, rather, made up of all age groups and backgrounds and they meet to pray, to celebrate the sacraments and to work for others. They therefore make up the basic Christian community of their area. Others who live in the area may come along to celebrate the Liturgy with them, or to lend a hand in some social work, but that doesn't make them members of the community. The community is characterised by the close personal commitment of the members to each other. The normal size is about twenty to thirty families, one hundred to one hundred and fifty people. They usually have their own meeting place, varying from the open palm

shelter I saw in Panama, to the substantial brick-built hall in the suburb
of Sao Paulo, Brazil. Though they run their own affairs completely
autonomously, they will normally have a priest who will celebrate the
Eucharist for them and give support in whatever ways he can.

Apart from simply describing what CEBs are, it is very important to
understand the new view of the Church and the new ways of living the
Gospel that they imply. It is a Brazilian priest, Jose Marins, who has
most clearly articulated these, and who is the leading authority in Latin
America on the CEBs. For Marins they can't be looked at as an isolated
fact. He sees the CEBs as a response "to the historical challenges which
the Church has been intensely living since Vatican II". He adds that
they exist "to question and change the models of existing society". He
goes on to draw out the implications:

> The main importance of the CEB isn't just that it is a new cell level
> of the Church . . . but that it inaugurates a new model of the Church.
> It isn't a new Church but it emphasises much more the missionary,
> communitarian and liberating aspects of the Church, offering believers
> a much greater and more effective participation in the life and mis-
> sion of the Church . . . It runs the risk of falling out with the rich
> through denouncing their injustices and all violations of human
> dignity but it conserves all the essential elements of being Church,
> insisting especially on being a Church serving and poor, committed
> and liberating, communitarian and personalising.[1]

The common experience all over Latin America is that CEBs have
grown up among the poor and marginalised. In many places the new
communities tend to be regarded with some hostility by the middle
classes, who are organised much more in the traditional movements like

the Saint Vincent de Paul Society, Christian Family Movement, Legion of Mary, and in the Charismatic Renewal. The 1978 Urban Pastoral Programme of the National Conference of Brazilian Bishops refers to this problem. "The majority of movements recruit their members from the middle classes," it says in the Section 2:5 on Forms of Ecclesial Communion, "and because the economic system in force favours these classes, it is difficult for the movements to question the social life of their members and to bring about a conversion to the perspectives of the poor. Often these movements serve the 'escapism' of those who want to call themselves 'devout' Catholics but who don't want to start asking questions about the problem of justice." In the urban situation today, where "traditional ecclesiastical structures are shown to be inadequate", the Brazilian bishops firmly side with the CEBs as new "forms of ecclesial communion", as they call them:

> The CEBs constitute the place for the conscientisation of the poor through a reflection on the problems of their life in the light of the Gospel in order to take decisions which will lead to action. Discovering the force which comes from unity, the CEBs are working to better the life of the local area through the common unity of the people. At times they work on their own; at times they participate in political activity to demand their rights at the level of the local area, of the city and, with the help of their pastors, right up to the national level.

The primary importance of the CEBs therefore lies firstly in the fact that they constitute the first structures the Church has found to incarnate itself in the urban situation, thus overcoming the horrifying gap between faith and life, the roots of which lie in the translation of a rural structure, the parish, to an urban situation. Important also is the fact that the Church is ceasing to be dominated by a minority of educated professionals, the clergy, and is becoming genuinely the People of God, concerned not with petty internal questions about its own organisation, but with the great issues which face the oppressed today. The CEBs therefore are not only important for church people, but for all those interested in the liberation of the oppressed. It is this aspect of them which Gary MacEoin, the well-known Irish American expert on Latin America, underlined recently:

> Brazil, originator of the theory and practice of neofascist dictatorship, was also the country in which the churches first took an open stand in opposition. To replace the social and religious organisations destroyed or domesticated by the regime, they developed a new way to organise, the 'grassroots community', a neighbourhood group often of twenty or fewer families. Committed to self-examination, conscientisation, dialogue and evaluation of possibilities, it is neither a church nor a civic organisation in traditional terms. The leader is

normally not a priest or a pastor. It is a community with its own indigenous leadership and a humanistic commitment.

In Brazil alone, they now number forty thousand or more, a network so autonomous and near invisible as to defy all attempts to destroy or domesticate. And wherever right wing terror has raged, in Chile, Argentina, Uruguay, Guatemala, El Salvador, Nicaragua and most recently Peru, so do the grassroots communities flourish, encouraged by Catholic priests and nuns, and by Protestant ministers, many of whom have testified in their blood to the cause of human dignity. Little known and less understood in the United States, the hemisphere-wide movement is the greatest threat to the established injustice, the greatest hope of a better tomorrow.[2]

If the theory seems well worked out, I found, in visiting communities in most of the Latin American countries, that the reality is a little more complex. There are very many places where communities which will broadly fit into the description elaborated above will not call themselves CEBs. More than once when I asked the question whether what I had seen could be called a CEB, I was given the answer: "If you want to call it that you can, but we don't". In a few cases I met some cynicism about the whole idea and was told by one priest who had spent seventeen years in Latin America that he had never seen or even heard about a real CEB in action!

CEBs in Action: Cuernavaca

Cuernavaca is a small, rather untypical city, forty miles south of Mexico City on the road to Acapulco. Because of its pleasant all-year round climate it is a favourite place for the rich of the capital to spend their week-ends, and has a large North American population who have come to retire there. Despite its pleasant exterior it too has its sprawling shanty towns; and it was for this reason that Pierre Roland, a French priest who had worked in Chile, came to Cuernavaca in 1966.

Living in a poor area, he began to get those people interested in their faith to come together once a week to read scripture and to discuss their response as Christians to the problems around them. Such groups began to spring up all over the city and soon there were more than eighty groups meeting each week. Looking back on it, one local priest describes it as "a real movement of decentralisation to construct a new type of parish." Anyone who has worked with basic communities stresses the distinctiveness of each one and the impossibility of adequately categorising them.

For Ray Plankey, a full time lay pastoral worker, who worked closely with such groups in Chile until the coup, and has continued to do so since in Cuernavaca, there is a common *raison d'etre* behind all such communities. They are not just a new movement within the church, but they have "all the basic properties of church." Thus they are a sign of the presence of Christ among men and women today; they show genuine love in practice; and they seek to turn outwards to do something effective about the problems of the larger community. They are not content to remain a ghetto. They constitute, therefore, a new type of parish or basic cell structure of the church.

In the ten years that they have flourished, Ray sees them as having gone through "a process of growing up". At first, he says, "they tended to go through a period of adolescence, of finding fulfillment in personal relationships." Now they have got beyond that to a social responsibility. Recently they have tended to become more and more politicised, as they become aware of the huge structural injustices around them. But, as Ray points out, "it is very difficult to find the balance between interior commitment to prayer and relationships and exterior commitment to political change." In Cuernavaca people from the basic communities have occupied the local municipal offices demanding that the City Council do more about the problems of the poor areas. In two of the poorest areas of the city, where the people live in shacks of corrugated iron, people associated with basic communities have started co-operatives, teaching skills like weaving or embroidery and trying to find market outlets for the goods the women make.

Just now Ray sees them as going through a crisis. Because of the radicalising process which has taken place some people drop out. Other communities cannot seem to break out of the endless rounds of discussion to get down to real action, and so they die out. Some see this as a healthy sign and as the training ground for a vanguard of really radically committed Christians in the future. Ray is sceptical, though. He feels the basic communities must extend further if they want to really effect change in society, so that they can relate more and more people to a genuine Christian community, and get more and more involved in the struggles of the poor.

I was lucky to witness the possible beginning of a basic community when I visited with Ray one poor *barrio* perched on two sides of a steep valley on the outskirts of Cuernavaca. Here we went to talk to twenty eight year old Carlos, trained as a vet, but living in very poor conditions earning a meagre income from a pig farm of some fifty pigs. "The people around here think me rich," he joked to us, but he explained that he supported his mother, two unmarried sisters with four children, a friend who has cancer, and his brother who has a broken finger at the moment. He showed us the X-ray photos of the brother's fingers as he told us this. We afterwards visited one of his sisters in her little hut perched on the side of the valley a few hundred yards from the pigs.

There Carlos began to show interest in getting together with others to discuss their faith and the problems of the *barrio* and try to organise people to do something about these problems. So he offered to get some people together and he would kill a pig the next Sunday for it. Ray promised to go and bring along another interested local man he knew. This prosaic event is the very way in which a basic community can begin, as Ray afterwards mentioned.

Though the growth and development of CEBs has been strongly supported by the bishop, Bishop Mendez Arceo (cf Chapter 7), the same cannot be said of all the priests of the diocese. In those parishes where the priest has been a support, the CEBs have been fully integrated into parish life and usually celebrate the Eucharist in the parish church on a Sunday, thus strengthening the larger parish community. In most cases however, the priests have been at best indifferent to the CEBs in their parish, and some have strongly denounced them from the pulpit. In these parishes they have usually found it impossible to develop, and have died out. In its section on CEBs Puebla referred to this problem when it said: "All this is a process, in which we still find broad sectors posing resistance of various sorts. This calls for understanding and encouragement, as well as great docility to the Holy Spirit. What we need now is still more clerical openness to the activity of the laity and the overcoming of pastoral individualism and self-sufficiency (par: 627)".

San Salvador

In the suburbs of San Salvador, the capital of the tiny Central American republic of El Salvador, I visited a big new working class housing estate with a population of about thirty thousand. Archbishop Romero had refused to break up the area, which is a natural unity, into territorial parishes. Instead, four priests went to live in the area supporting the people in setting up a network of CEBs based in the blocks of flats. This network has developed spontaneously, with each CEB electing a co-ordinator who meets weekly with the co-ordinators of the five or six CEBs of the immediate block of flats, who themselves send a co-ordinator to a weekly central meeting. Maria, herself a co-ordinator in her early twenties and living in one of the flats, emphasised as she explained this elaborate structure to me, that it wasn't worked out in theory and then applied to the situation, but that it had evolved naturally.

One of the difficulties they have had to face is that two of the priests of the area have been expelled, and in January, 1979, another was shot dead in cold blood by the police together with four teenagers of the area while holding a day retreat with them. Though they have been badly shaken by the killing, they see it as a sign that they are truly living the Gospel. As Archbishop Romero said to me: "Where there is no persecution, there is no church — it is one of the necessary marks of being a Christian." To me another sign of the strength and vitality of their faith was, that even though the killings had taken place less than two months before I visited them, they had already written a hymn about it which they sang at the meetings I attended:

> Forward with all our force,
> Let us put an end to our sadness,
> Our five brothers are calling us
> to follow and struggle;
> we must get up.
> Don't ever leave aside our ideals,
> cry out to us the martyrs of Deespertar.
>
> *Refrain:* Enough, Enough,
>   Enough of Death and Falsity,
>   Enough, Enough,
>   is the cry in San Antonio Abad.

Despite the lack of priests, the communities continue their work, strengthened by the example of their martyred brothers. A Lenten reflection which the co-ordinators had prepared for the use of the CEBs, which we discussed at the meetings, asked the following questions:

Does our Christian faith strengthen us for our political commitment?
Are we violent (active, decisive) with respect to our pastoral work?
Do we have enough prayer, enough commitment in our life?
What do our martyrs mean for me in my life?

The closing hymn we sang summed up the strength of these CEBs and their effect on the people:

> When the poor believe in the poor,
> Then we can sing Liberty,
> When the poor believe in the poor,
> We will build up brotherhood.

Panama

The semi-urban, semi-rural area of Las Cumbres in the outskirts of Panama City presents a different picture. This is a long established parish with two churches which has been swamped by the influx of country people looking for work. The four Spanish Dominicans who live in the area decided to move out of their house next to the parish church in an effort to de-emphasise the church as the centre of the Christian community. Instead, they have supported the growth of CEBs all over the area. The traditional parish functions only to the extent of providing one Mass every Sunday in each of the two churches for those "who want an easy and automatic Christianity which makes no de-mands," as Juan, one of the priests, put it. This is the traditional reli-gion of the middle class people who dominated the area before the influx of poor from the country.

But it is among these poor that the new church "born of the people" is growing. Serving the seven CEBs of the area are twenty-nine lay ministers, mostly young people who are licensed by the archbishop and who lead the liturgy in each of the communities every Sunday, baptis-ing, ministering Holy Communion, and acting as a go-between with the priests, calling one in whenever is necessary. Each CEB celebrates the Eucharist once a month, which is as often as one of the priests can get around to each of them.

As well as this, there is a group of about twenty catechists, again young local people, who have worked out their own programme of preparation for First Communion, Confirmation and Marriage. They meet each Saturday afternoon to discuss their work for the next week. What struck me, the Saturday I sat in on one of their meetings, was their competence in elaborating and carrying out an education pro-gramme for some hundreds of adults and children. While this pro-gramme at the moment is an extension of a catechetical programme which the government have recently allowed be introduced into the schools, it is expected that it will soon by the only religious education for the young people of the area. As one of the priests, Miguel, who worked on preparing the schools programme, told me: "The govern-ment will soon stop the schools programme when they see just how aware it is making the pupils of the realities of society here."

I visited the weekly meetings of two CEBs, held under shelters of palm leaves. There were some twenty five to thirty adults at each of the meetings, young and old, men and women, with children running around freely. We read Scripture, prayed, and listened to an old man telling us how he was being harrassed by Americans and prevented from planting on his little bit of land because it was just inside the boundary of the Canal Zone which had been set aside for afforestation. A middle-aged woman handed around some dolls she had made out of simple materials which she intended to take to town and sell to make a small income. At the end the leader, a woman, prayed for the coming of the Kingdom where the oppressed like themselves will be fully liberated. I was afterwards told that officials had visited some of these CEBs, threatening them because they were taking surveys of all the people who had no water, light of sewerage in their simple homes. As Puebla said: "The basic community is an expression of the church's preferential love for the poor" to whom it "affords the concrete possibility of participation in the church's task, and in the commitment to transform the world." (par. 643).

Santiago

Chile was one of the first countries to develop the basic community in the late sixties, and the suburb of Villa Portales in Santiago is a well organised example. A housing complex of 1,943 flats with over 15,000 inhabitants, it has about five hundred activists involved in the various CEBs of the area. One young member, Pablo, expresses what the community means to him: "In the community I have been enriched personally, I have discovered new dimensions of friendship. In prayer and in commitment to my brothers I've grown as a man." Max, in charge of the pre-baptismal *Pastoral** has a slightly different emphasis: "We haven't prepared ourselves for ourselves but to serve others. To serve our suffering brother, the most needy, is the mission Christ entrusted to the Church."

To do this, CEBs are organised in two groups, adults and youth. The adult groups, formed mostly of married couples, comprise a solidarity team, teams for pre-baptismal and pre-marriage Pastoral, a team for caring for the sick, and one for catechetics. One member put it this way: "We are committed to the spiritual formation of the people. But we also pay attention to their material needs." Therefore they run a daily *comedor* bringing meals to over eighty needy families, an old peoples' club and a solidarity fund to help people unable to pay their bills, or for necessary medical attention.

The young are organised into information groups, which firstly prepare children for their First Communion, and then continue their preparation through their teens for a more active involvement in the community. They run a library, which not only makes books available to students, but also helps them with problems. "For this we depend on the help of university students and teachers," said Sophia, who is in

---

*I use the word *pastoral* as it is normally used in Latin America, namely as a noun. Its meaning is much fuller than the English adjective 'pastoral'. It denotes a planned process with clearly established aims and means which can then be evaluated in the light of results. A specific *pastoral*, such as preparing people for baptism, will normally be part of a wider process at the level of a basic community or a parish. This local *pastoral* will then fit into a diocesan *pastoral* or even into a national one.

charge of the library. The bulletin team publishes a monthly information leaflet for all the area. Another team organises retreats, meetings, and courses for young people.

To keep all this activity going there is an administration group to co-ordinate and maintain the various activities and centres. Fr Fernando, the pastor of the local parish, emphasises that all this took "two or three years of intense activity. It doesn't happen overnight." Even with this level of organisation and activity, the CEBs of Villa Portales are not satisfied. Alicia, one of the leaders, said: "We want our Christian Community to be present wherever there is need. Recently the people of Villa Portales have formed a board to administer the area. The community is present in that. Two of our neighbours, mother and son, have been detained for taking part in the May Day parade. The community is present in that. We want to be with all and for all."

She finished off by mentioning a problem that is not unique to Chile: "Many still have very little concern for the problems of others. They want to live apart in their flats without looking at the world around them. Our duty as Christians is to go to them, opening ourselves to them, so that they also can open themselves to the community, to all the community."

A community which brings their problems right to the heart of their weekly liturgy is in Villa Prudencia, a working class estate of high rise flats where the people are suffering badly due to the economic policies of the military government. With a high level of unemployment, many of the men have to join the daily queues on *empleo minima,* the government's substitute for unemployment benefit. Under this system the workers have to accept whatever tasks they are given each day, usually heavy physical labour. For this they are paid a rate of £15.00 a month, half of which, it is estimated, goes on transport costs to and from their work.

Fr Jose lives in a simple wooden shack among these high rise flats, and shares daily in the workers' lives even to the extent of working on the *empleo minima.* Every Sunday, the Christian community crowd into another wooden shack in the middle of a patch of waste ground, and bring their struggles and hopes to their liturgical celebration. Three Sundays out of four, this is led by a group of the people themselves, with Jose playing his accordion in the corner; on one Sunday a month, he celebrates the Eucharist with them.

He told me that his decision not to celebrate the Eucharist every day or even every Sunday was a most painful one for him, but one he felt he had to make if he was really to be part of this community, sharing their life and struggles. "I also felt afraid when I had to leave my family, my world, and involve myself in another, very distinct world," he says of his decision to leave the security and comfort of the diocesan seminary where he had taught. "But Jesus became one of us to make us free, to struggle for the liberation of the people."

The weekly liturgy allows the people to express their deepest hopes and needs in a way no other public meeting in Chile today could. The Sunday I attended they read from Exodus, Chapter 3, on the call of Moses to lead the people of Israel out of their slavery. This they applied to their own slavery under the military dictatorship and their struggles to organise against it. For over two and a half hours they prayed, reflected with periods of quiet, recounted experiences, and expressed their needs or those of their families and friends. All this was interspersed with regular bouts of hearty singing. Afterwards, since it was the feast of St Michael, we all went around to the flats of three men called Miguel and, accompanied by Jose on the accordion, sang them a song outside their window, wishing them happy feast day.

These CEBs in Santiago are a good example of what Marins counts as being one of their most distinctive qualities: "the diminuition in work exclusively ecclesial and the collaboration in the work of the human community of the area, co-operating in projects with other groups."[3]

Engaging in such projects has led members of CEBs to realise their need to analyse and understand the basic injustices and inequalities in society. Not resting content to deal with the symptoms they seek to get to the root of social problems. The means to do this is conscientisation.

Chapter Three

CONSCIENTISATION:
INSISTING ON TRUTH

"But we have his promise, and look forward to new heavens and a new earth, the home of justice."

2 Peter 3:13

"In the developing countries the principal aim of this education for justice consists in an attempt to awaken consciences to a knowledge of the concrete situation and in a call to secure a total improvement: by these means the transformation of the world has already begun."

Synod of Bishops: Justice in the World

If basic communities provide the means for people to become the subjects of their history rather than being, as formerly, the objects of outside manipulation, the process of conscientisation creates the necessary consciousness. From its beginnings, by Paulo Freire in the Northeast of Brazil in the early sixties, the methods and theory of a liberating education have been developed and applied in different ways in many parts of Latin America. This chapter firstly examines the theory behind conscientisation, a theory rarely understood and more often misapplied in the developed world. It then gives three examples of its application. The first example shows the process used in a liturgical context, both as to the content of the liturgy and in weekly leaflets for liturgical use; it comes from Brazil. Also from Brazil is the second example of catechetics used as a means for conscientising. The third example shows how a whole diocese can fulfil a conscientising role for a society; it is the diocese of San Salvador, capital of El Salvador.

Paulo Freire: Conscientisation in Theory

When Freire was professor of education at the University of Recife in the early sixties, he saw clearly that traditional means for teaching literacy only perpetuated the dependent situation of the poor. At best it taught poor people the means to better themselves so that, as Freire says, "for them the new man is themselves become oppressors. Their vision of the new man is individualistic; because of their identification with the oppressor, they have no consciousness of themselves as persons or as members of an oppressed class."[1] To move beyond this "banking concept of education which domesticates", Freire evolved a "problem-posing education which involves a constant unveiling of reality . . . striving for the emergence of consciousness and critical intervention in reality."[2]

This he did by using themes from the culture of the oppressed, whether in an urban or a rural context. Thus words like *favela,* slum, or *trabalho,* work, were used as a mirror of the people's real life situation instead of the usual text-books using images from a middle-class world. With *favela* would go a slide or drawing of poor housing, and this theme would ask questions such as : "Do all Brazilians have adequate houses? Where and why do they lack houses? Is the system of savings and loans sufficient for acquiring a house?" Similarly a photo of a factory with a 'No Jobs' sign provides the context for a discussion on employment and industrialisation. Through this method Freire was able both to teach the language tools for looking at and expressing the people's own reality, and also to help them value their own culture and capabilities.

Becoming aware of the oppressive reality and its causes leads to action to change it. "As we expose the oppressive situation, we are forced to a decision," Freire says, "we either commit ourselves or we don't. As I conscientise myself, I realise that my brothers who don't eat, who don't laugh, who don't sing, who don't love, who live oppressed, crushed and despised, who are less each day, are suffering all this because of some reality that is causing it, and at that point I join in the action historically by genuinely loving, by having the courage to commit myself, or I end up with a sense of guilt because I am not doing what I know I should."[3]

Freire realises that conscientisation "involves an excruciating moment, a tremendously upsetting one, the moment when one starts to be re-born and to understand others." Many seek to escape from the task of changing society "by almsgiving, I send a cheque, I make contributions." But, Freire goes on, "peace cannot be purchased, I cannot live my peace without commitment to people and my commitment to people can't exist without their liberation, and liberation can't exist without the final transformation of the structures that are dehumanising them."[4]

Conscientisation, then, is "political, just as political as the education which claims to be neutral, although actually serving the power elite." Therefore, one cannot naively try to apply it within the existing structures of education, Freire emphasises: "Truly liberating education can only be put into practice outside the ordinary system, and even then with great cautiousness, by those who overcome their naiveness and commit themselves to authentic liberation."⁵

So a commitment to conscientisation implies a rejection of the traditional educational structures which can only function to perpetuate the existing oppressing society, no matter how many new and experimental methods and curricula may be introduced. Basic communities and the various church organisations that are committed to liberation now provide the structures for a conscientising education. In fact, it can be said that basic communities themselves are a result of oppressed people becoming aware, due to conscientisation, and discovering their own power and worth.

For Freire, one of the results of commitment to a liberating education for many Christians is that "they encounter risks formerly unknown. When they had engaged in purely palliative action, they were praised for their Christian virtues. But when they begin to see the need for a house, free employment, bread, clothing, health, and education for their children, they find their very faith being called into question. They are denounced as serving an international demonic force which threatens 'Western Christian civilisation', a civilisation which, in reality, has very little that is Christian about it."⁶ Our first example illustrates this vividly.

Brazil: Conscientising through Liturgy

Though a separate diocese, Nova Iguacu is in effect an enormous suburb for Rio de Janeiro, with a population of some two million. Dom Adriano Hypolito, the bishop, uses the printed weekly leaflet called *A Folha* for Masses all over the diocese as a means for conscientising. The two following extracts come from that of 29th July 1979. The first is headed "Investigation of the Clergy", and prints extracts from a document which had just come to light, with criticism by *A Folha* at the end.

"Taking account of the increasing denunciations which showed a growing leftwing radicalization of the Catholic Church — denunciations made above all by the organs of military security — President Geisel in the first days of his presidency in March 1974 asked the Minister of Justice to make a complete investigation into the situation. The results set out certain serious conclusions. One of these accused the clergy of being 'the most active of our enemies, promoting, by clearly subversive means, the substitution of the Brazilian political, social and economic structure by a new order, in every way similar to Marxist philosophy.' The authors of the document were especially disturbed by the 'vast organization of the communist clergy subordinated to the CNBB (National Conference of Brazilian Bishops),' remembering that the Church can count on, for communicating its message, 5,577 parishes, 276 bishops, 12,647 priests, 42,671 other religious, 143 third level colleges, 68 radio stations, 82 magazines and 4 television channels.

"The Centre for Information and Security of the Air Force, divided into five items the points which, according to their anonymous analyst, 'indicate most clearly the activity of elements of the communist clergy: (1) The conscientisation of the least favoured classes in their rights. (2) The negation of capitalism as an indirect way to condemn political regimes. (3) Submission to left-wing jargon. (4) Excessive zeal in defending members of the clergy caught up in subversive ideology. (5) The lack of authority in the church to curb the excesses of its members.'

"It is lamentable that public money is spent on this type of service. The ex-President ought to have ordered also an investigation into tortures, deaths and the selling of Brazil to foreign companies. For the Bishop of Nova Iguacu, Dom Adriano Hypolito, the government can investigate the activity of the clergy as often as it likes, 'because the church hasn't a position of inviolability and it isn't afraid. What is to be condemned is the false interpretation put on certain facts. But whenever the church decides on the defence of justice against injustice, of the poor against the rich, of the weak against the strong and whenever the people commit themselves to a more just social order, then we can only expect this type of misinterpretation.'"

The second extract is their regular comment on recent events in an ironic style, applying them to the people's situation:

"Speaking of the visit the Chancellor of the Federal Republic of Germany made to Brazil recently, our morning papers made their usual, just, and reasonable comments. And with that elitist tone we can always count on.

"They take up the theme of the Third World. According to Chancellor Schmidt, Brazil ought to assume the leadership of that Third World. The leaderwriters were talking about a Brazilian vocation because of our open society, our market economy, our capitalism with state regulations, which has such a social conscience that it realises the evils that can result from too much state power.

"But the learned leaderwriters who write such erudite commentaries can afford to mix themselves up more than the people can. They have the chance to modify their position. But the people are profoundly marginalized, thanks to the elites in power. The people don't have a second chance.

"A Brazilian vocation — or a vocation of the economic, political and military elites? If we look at Brazil yesterday and today we can see that the people are more marginalized today than yesterday. This marginalization hinders the Brazilian having any vocation. That is the reality."

From the huge rural parish of Rubim in the state of Minas Gerais, one of the oldest states of Brazil, comes an example of conscientising through the content of the liturgy itself. Because the parish is some sixty miles long by twenty-five miles wide, the two priests and four sisters make out weekly liturgical services which the rural basic communities can use on the Sundays when a priest cannot come to celebrate the Eucharist. Though the land in this area is good, it is all owned by big landowners who can make more profit by using it to graze cattle than for growing food. Therefore people go hungry despite all the good land around them, and many have to migrate to the cities.

The liturgy takes up this experience of the people helping them to see the true cause of their poverty. The following text was used by a group of some sixty people, men women and children, who met under a shelter of palm leaves erected next to a tiny school. Though the nearest town was only about an hour away the road was almost non-existent in parts. We arrived with some difficulty in a jeep but the locals all came on horseback. They were mostly poor farm labourers, the majority in their twenties and thirties, used to a life of insecurity and resignation. The message of the liturgy spoke directly to their needs and they listened with attention, the men at the back, the women and children at the front. At times they threw in their own comments showing a deep perceptiveness about the relevance of the Gospel to their situation. It was Sunday 22nd April, 1979, the Sunday after Easter Sunday.

The liturgy opens with a hymn and greeting after which is an introduction to the theme of the day:

Last Sunday we celebrated the Resurrection of Jesus. With his Resurrection, Jesus wants the people too to live like risen people. The happenings of bibilical times musn't seem to us very distant. In our family and our community we recognise the Resurrection every time a person begins to live a better life, whether in body or spirit. It is about this that we are going to reflect and pray today.

After a Prayer comes the First Reading called: *The Evidence of a Worker:*

A Sao Paulo worker says on the occasion of a strike: 'The worker is only a cog in the machine of production. Both the peasant and the industrial worker have no status in society. And why not? Simply because some decide that things ought to be so. They never ask us. This set-up doesn't come from us, it comes from those above us. I think it's very important that the urban worker and the rural workers must participate in the political life of the country with representatives, with the right of association, the circulation of ideas, with factory committees and free trade unions. The worker must participate because he produces everything.

Then comes another hymn and the introduction to the Second Reading, from James 5: 1–6:

The Bible reading today speaks very seriously to us about the rich. It seems that God too, doesn't like the rich. It is important for you to remember that the rich the Bible condemns are those who are egotistical, and who oppress the weak; just as you all know many weak people can exploit those weaker than themselves.

The reading is followed by points for reflection:

Is the Sao Paulo worker right when he speaks as he does? Has the rural situation similarities with that of the Sao Paulo worker? What, for example? Is God, who is our Father, satisfied that the rich exploit the poor?

There follows an addition entitled, "Additional Points to Help the Leader, (can be read out if necessary):

The Church is very clear in its position. It doesn't condemn anyone. Its mission is to denounce all that goes against the marvellous plans of God our Father. It is against all injustice, all exploitation, all oppression of man by man. Continuing the commentary of our courageous worker of Sao Paulo, we are told: 'The fact is that the value of work is not being respected. The workers make up 80% of the people. Those who own the machinery and the land are scarcely 5%. All the workers together earn eight times less than this rich 5%. This is what it means: where the worker earns 1 cruzeiro for his work, the rich person earns 128 cruzeiros. In a country where this can happen it is clear that the value of work isn't being respected as it ought to be. And how has this come about? The land was taken from the worker and because of this his work can be exploited by the owner of the land . . .

This leads into the Rite of Pardon, the Our Father, the Communion and after it, the Final Blessing. At the end of the liturgy comes 'Information to be read following the Liturgy':

Because we are reflecting about the rights and duties of all, we are going to read something more about this. What is a trade union? Here is an exchange which every militant repeats many times to his comrades. Are you a member of a trade union? No. Why not? Because the trade union does nothing for me. If everyone who thinks like this remains outside it, how is the trade union going to be improved?

A trade union is an organisation where the workers defend their interests and fight for justice. The trade union fights for better salaries, better conditions of work, for a new society. In this fight it must either confront or ally itself with other sectors of society, such as employers, the Church, political parties, students, associations, clubs, etc. This is as it is in other countries. Here in Brazil it is different. The laws are of such a kind that the comrades think the trade union is an organ of government. The trade union is the people; next Sunday we will talk about certain laws concerning duties and rights of trade unionists and all rural workers."

Sao Paulo: Conscientising through Catechetics

Catechetics, or religious education, is also a means used for opening the people's eyes. In Itaquera which is one of the poorest suburbs of Sao Paulo, 89% of households lack running water, 96% lack drains, 71% lack refuse collection; and most of the streets are unpaved dust tracks. The basic communities of the area have evolved their own catechetical programme, applying the Gospel to the needs of the people.

The programme, called *The Kingdom of God is Among Us,* is a series of reflections on the New Testament, in thirty sections. Each section has a scriptural passage together with questions on it, and finishes with activities. Each section also has a drawing to illustrate it, underlining the meaning of the text, or applying it to the reality of the people's lives. The programme is designed to be used by a family, and therefore is directed as much at adults as it is at children. Once a week the trained catechist meets with a group of leaders to go over a section of the catechetical programme. Each member of this group then meets with a further group to familiarise them with the topic. The members of this group then bring the message home to their families. The introduction, therefore, emphasises that the programme should not be used in a "scholarly style", but as an aid to begin a discussion based on the people's own experience of life.

I sat in on a group of nine women meeting with the catechist one afternoon. This group meets in each other's homes and, that particular afternoon, they were discussing the section: "Jesus was born poor and partook fully in our life." After reading Luke's account of the birth of Jesus, we discussed the questions: "What happens in a family when a new child is born? Do you think that the life of every child has a value, or have some more value than others? If Jesus was so fully involved in life, what did he want to teach us by his birth?

The discussion went naturally from the question of Jesus being born poor to stories of how the women felt they were treated badly because they are poor: They are kept waiting in the pharmacy; when they are at work, they are only allowed a particular chair to sit in; when they were young, they never had milk. Jesus was born poor, they said, to show the dignity of the poor. Then does God wish poverty? No, poverty is man made, we must struggle to change it.

This section, then, fits into the overall programme, the theme of which is set out in the object of the first section: "We understand that God wants to build a Kingdom of love, justice and peace with all of us, and for this Jesus came; so that all people could have an ever better life in every sense of the word." Each section highlights different aspects building up to a greater awareness of the people's own dignity and the need to be involved in the struggles to change society.

The section on the Good Samaritan asks the question: "At work, in your suburb, in the city, what are the problems that people have created?" In considering Jesus the worker, there is an activity asking which of the following list of the products of their labour do they themselves possess: beans, an apartment, warm clothes, cars, colour TV, running water, bread, armchairs, carpets, a fridge? They are then asked to write why they cannot possess more than they do. The section 'Jesus affirms that all are brothers' asks what is the minimum wage, and whether this shows that people are treated as brothers. 'Jesus uses the goods of the earth' is illustrated by a drawing showing a man claiming all the land as his own. Another replies, "The land doesn't belong to any one person but to all." One of the questions in this section asks simply, "Why are there rich people and people who have nothing?" The object of another section is: "To live without domination and oppression." The section on false prophets is applied to advertising on TV, in magazines and on hoardings: "What do these advertisements want? What is a consumer society?" Another illustration shows a boss giving out to a worker who is thinking: "The boss earns five times more than I do, and yet he gives out to me all day. Why should he have more rights than I do?" The final sections ask: "What are the major problems the people have? Why do they exist? What are you going to do? Do you have a group or community you can participate in?"

Another catechetical method for adults is called *Circulos Biblicos,* Bible circles. As in the catechetical programme, a leader will take a group once a week. Each member will then act as leader in another group in his own area. The text is taken from weekly printed sheets produced in Sao Paulo. Each has an Old Testament and a New Testament reading with questions, and each reflection is preceded by a "Text from life" a little story illustrating some problems of the people. It can be rising prices, pollution problems caused by lack of filters on local factories, a refuse collector who was too poor to buy gloves or boots. The questions then take up these situations: "What are our communities doing to help the needy? How can we share the goods of the earth more equally?"

These and other ways of building up people's consciousness prepare the people to take action when the opportunity arises. One such opportunity arose when a group got together to demand that the railway company put up safety barriers: In a three-month period forty people had been killed crossing the tracks. When they got no satisfaction from a meeting with representatives of the company, the local bishop Dom Angelico Bernardino stopped all Masses in his region one Sunday and led the people to sit on the tracks until they got what they wanted. The railway company had to give in.

The process of conscientisation is helping oppressed people find a dignity they have never known, and discover a solidarity with one another. For these people, simply uncovering the mechanisms of oppression in society, and how these operate against them is itself liberating action. "This is the commitment of the church in the class struggle," Dom Angelico told me, "forming the unity of the working class divided by the capitalist system, and replacing an individualistic mentality with a class mentality."

San Salvador: A Church takes sides

Television film of the killing of twenty-four people by the military on the steps of the Cathedral of San Salvador at the beginning of May, 1979, gave many people all over the world their first introduction to the tiny Central American republic of El Salvador. The increasing slide into civil war between the Left and Right which has brought international attention to El Salvador, has also highlighted the role of Don Oscar Romero, Archbishop of the capital from February 1977 to his assassination in March 1980. This role was summed up by a man who spoke from the audience at the end of a press conference in Puebla. After telling us he was an exile from El Salvador because of his political work for social change, and a non-believer, he offered solidarity and support to the archbishop in "the heroic struggle which he has undertaken for the rights and necessities of the people."

Archbishop Romero did not come to this role easily. Criticised by some of his priests when he was made archbishop for being too conservative, he has "allowed himself be transformed by the history of his people," as one priest put it to me. "It took him many years and a lot of suffering to find a structural place for the church within a situation of violence, and many months of discussion with theologians and social scientists."

Out of this effort to get to the roots of the causes of violence in his country, the archbishop came to certain conclusions, conclusions which he ever more insistently underlined as the violence escalated in El Salvador. There are expressed in a Pastoral Letter, *The Church and Popular Political Organizations,* published in August 1978. "The most widespread form of violence in our continent as well as in our country," he said, "is what the bishops at Medellin called 'institutionalised violence', the product of a situation of injustice in which the majority of men and women, and above all of children, are deprived of the basic necessities for life."

These words take on particular meaning when it is remembered that 8% of the population share 50% of the national income, while 92% have to make do with the other 50%. The 60% of the population who live on the land have to eke out a seasonal living, working for less than £1 a day during the four to six month harvest season. Therefore it is not surprising that 57% of Salvadoreans are illiterate, and that three out of every five children suffer from malnutrition.

The archbishop went on: "The violence is expressed in the organisation and daily functioning of a socio-economic and political system which accepts as normal and everyday that progress isn't possible without the majority being utilised as a productive force by a privileged minority. We always meet this type of violence when the institutional mechanisms function for the benefit of a minority and systematically discriminate against groups and persons who defend the genuine common good."

The security forces have been used to maintain this system, which caused El Salvador to be condemned by the Organisation of American States early in 1979 for "extremely cruel and inhuman conditions of detention" and for the use of "physical and psychological torture and mistreatment." The archbishop mentioned this also when he spoke of "the repressive violence of the security forces of the state when they try to restrain the desires of the majority, putting down any manifestation of protest against the injustice which we have talked about."

This insistent uncovering of the true nature of Salvadorean society ran as a thread through the work of the archdiocese. It found its main expression in the weekly sermon of the archbishop at his 8.00 a.m. Mass in the cathedral every Sunday. An example was the sermon of 21st January, 1979, which was also the funeral Mass of a priest and four young people shot dead by the military the day before.

Preaching on these murders, the archbishop said: "The diocese declares that the official communication published in the media is a lie from beginning to end." He then read out an eye-witness account of the killings. This showed clearly that the five were murdered in cold blood and that there was no truth in the military allegations that they had been armed. Archbishop Romero concluded: "We are day by day losing faith in government and the media of communication. We are now obliged to rely on international publications and organisations because we can't rely on the justice and truth of our own. Above all a purification of the corrupt system of the security forces of our country is urgent". And, he went on, "We have had enough. I say this to you, not with pessimism, but with a great optimism in the strength of our people . . . who are capable of getting to the roots of our evils and realising the radical and urgent changes necessary in our society." The archbishop then pronounced a canonical excommunication on "those materially and intellectually responsible for the assassination of the priest, Octavio Ortiz."

After reflecting on the three readings of the Mass, the archbishop finished, as he did every Sunday, with the "Events of the Week." He appealed for information on the whereabouts of a man who had disappeared; he appealed for the release of two English and a Japanese who had been kidnapped; and he referred to the occupation of the offices of the Red Cross and the Organisation of American States, as well as the Mexican Embassy, by a guerilla group, FAPU. "This showed," he said, "the lack of freedom of expression in the country because of which they had to take these measures to have their voice listened to and to which the security forces reacted in a brutal and inflexible way."

Finally, that Sunday, the archbishop referred to a report that the President of El Salvador had said there was no persecution of the church there. "The bodies that are here in this cathedral show what a liar he is," he replied sharply. "And I'll say to finish: I insist that the conflict isn't between the church and the government, it is between the government and the people. The church is with the people and the people are with the church."

This consistent uncovering of truth and standing for justice was backed up by the diocesan radio station and weekly newspaper, *Orientacion*. The radio station's most popular programme of the week, which had one of the highest number of listeners of any radio programme in the country, was the live broadcast of the archbishop's Sunday sermon. The head of the station told me that "99.9% of our philosophy is that of the church: to defend human rights."

When the police opened fire on a peaceful demonstration in support of a strike in the centre of San Salvador while I was there, the church's radio station, out of more than seventy stations in the country, was the only one to report what had happened. The station was blown up by a bomb planted by a Right-wing group, at the end of February 1980.

The weekly *Orientacion* is also openly critical of the government. As well as weekly analyses of government legislation and policy, it carries a page called *Solidaridad*. This gives details of disappeared people, of bodies found mutilated and tortured, of strikes, and of the activities of the security forces and of a Right-wing para-military group called *Orden*. As a practical expression of solidarity the diocese has an office for judicial help through which people who have disappeared, been tortured or otherwise violated can have their cases brought up in the courts.

Archbishop Romero's courageous insistence on social change came under increasing attack by representatives of the ruling class. I saw editorials in the daily newspapers accusing the archbishop of being the cause of the country's troubles because of his preaching. An indication of the lengths to which this opposition goes is that a magazine called *La Opinion* devoted almost all its space to discrediting him. One issue accused the archbishop of being a hypocrite and of not paying the employees of the archdiocesan organisation *Caritas,* a just wage. Another article was headed: "Despite Mons. Romero fomenting it, the Pope condemns class struggle"; and in another he was called "Marx-nulfo Romero". The editorial counselled: "Humility ought to be the virtue of a good pastor", and accused Archbishop Romero of making "his words and conduct an expression of vanity and conceit." In an advertisement copied from one of San Salvador's dailies, the church was accused of being used by the USSR to spread Marxism. "Marxist doctrines," it said, "based on class hatred and violence, which are contrary to the Christian spirit of social harmony and peace, are taught from Catholic pulpits and in Catholic universities."

In the face of this, Archbishop Romero remained adamant. He told me: "The church must denounce injustice, or to put it better, it must announce justice, it must call people to a change of heart. The church isn't responsible for their being no change in society: it's those who don't hear the demand of the church for change who are to blame. It isn't preaching justice which is subversive, but maintaining situations which are unjust."

Archbishop Romero paid the ultimate price when he was assassinated saying Mass on March 24th 1980. Because of his work he had known that his life was in danger. But for him the people came first. In the final major interview he gave two weeks before his death he admitted that "in difficult moments we all suffer fear, the instinct for self-preservation is very strong, and for that I ask help. Help not only for me, but for all those who are carrying out this pastoral work, that we might remain at our posts because we have much to do . . . the flame of social justice must always remain alight in the hearts of the Salvadorean people."[7]

Chapter Four

ORGANISATIONS:
SUPPORTING THE PEOPLE'S STRUGGLES

"And his gifts were that some should be apostles, some prophets, some evangelists, some pastors and teachers, to equip the saints for the work of ministry, for building up the body of Christ, until we all attain to the unity of the faith and of the knowledge of the Son of God, to mature manhood, to the measure of the stature of the fulness of Christ."

Ephesians 4:11-13

"Unless the Christian message of love and justice shows its effectiveness through action in the cause of justice in the world, it will only with difficulty gain credibility with the men of our times."

Synod of Bishops: Justice in the World

The organisation of the people in basic communities and the process of conscientisation, which makes them aware of oppression, have posed a challenge to the wider organizations of the church. Where this challenge has been taken up, the traditional structures of the church, such as parishes, dioceses and even episcopal conferences, have totally reorganized themselves to support the popular movements. To illustrate this I will take the example of Brazil, of its pastoral planning at a national level, and of the implementation of this in the archdiocese of Sao Paulo, and particularly in one of its parishes, Vila Alpina.

Apart from the re-orientation of the traditional structures, totally new church organizations have grown up in response to local needs. Such an organization is the Vicariate of Solidarity of the Archdiocese of Santiago, Chile, responding as it is to the people's situation since the military coup of September 1973; it is my second example. Finally the Panamanian Centre of Studies and Social Action in Panama City, which provides background studies and research into questions affecting Panama's social and economic life, is my third example.

Pastoral planning in Brazil:

For many Latin Americans, the idea of pastoral action has taken on totally new meanings. The Puebla document says that the church must help "to construct a new society in complete fidelity to Christ and humanity." "To concretely carry out these fundamental pastoral options," the bishops stress the need for "a well-planned pastoral effort." (pars 1305/6)

It is the Brazilian Church which has developed most fully this process of pastoral planning. Starting with the National Plans of the National Conference of Brazilian Bishops (CNBB), many dioceses then elaborate their own plans which are put into practice in different ways in each sector, parish and community.

A good example of such planning at national level is the report of the Co-Ordinators of the Pastoral of the Large Cities, a group of bishops of the fifteen largest cities of the country together with specialists in theology, sociology, anthropology and history, and published at the end of 1978 as part of the Fourth Biannual Plan of the CNBB. Called *Approaches towards an Urban Pastoral*, the report begins by trying to "face up with objectivity to the reality of life in our cities."

The first half of the report is devoted to an analysis of the underlying trends of urban life in Brazil today. Beginning with the rapid growth of cities since 1940 (by 1980 two thirds of the population will live in cities) the authors pin-point some of the most disquieting aspects of this growth. "An economic model of industrialization with the participation of multinational companies and the imposition of forms of political authoritarianism in our society," has led, they say, to "accentuated social injustice and provoked a hardening of the conflict between oppressors and oppressed . . . leading to a clear division of classes." Due to this situation, the church "is conscious of the necessity for definitive options and has principally assumed the 'perspective of the poor' because the dimension of justice and the integral liberation of people is a constituent of the Gospel and the mission of the church."

From the standpoint of this clear perspective, many other familiar problems are touched upon. Cities show a division between a rich centre, which means "areas of concentration of power, of money and of all the services and benefits which they attract," and a 'periphery', "areas of accumulating misery lacking in all essential services" which are so visible surrounding all Brazil's cities. Later on in the report "the promotion of justice and more human conditions in the periphery" is further mentioned as a priority of the church's pastoral action.

Another problem clearly outlined is the anonymity of modern cities, which, in treating people *en masse*, makes them "prisoners to the game of a consumer society" leading to an "insensitivity to injustice and inequality." In this situation "traditional ecclesiastical structures – dioceses, parishes and chapels – which were developed for a rural situation . . . are shown to be inadequate to create community in the urban setting." This has led to the growth of "movements, groups and basic communities." Far from merely welcoming these, the first half of the report ends with the challenge: "It isn't enough simply to allow the peaceful co-existence of these diverse structures, but they must be brought together 'in a mutual and fruitful cooperation in the search for new structures."

The second part of the report details how some of these new structures should evolve. Called *Planning Pastoral Action on the Basis of the Urban Reality*, it firmly stresses the need for "the effective participation of the people in taking decisions about their pastoral action" so that "planning won't be executed by directives from above or outside the Christian community but will be a co-ordination of the common efforts of all."

Hence the traditional social-work type approach of trying to solve problems for people which only keeps them dependent on outside agencies and passive with regard to their own environment, is sharply criticised. Instead, "it is the people themselves who should assume actively their own history," and the wider church should put at their disposal, particularly at the disposal of the "most marginalized and undefended, all their human, moral and material resources." The means listed for doing this are the defence of prisoners and the victims of arbitrary treatment, juridical help for the defence of workers' rights, support for popular movements against such things as forced slum clearances, information and popular education which would help people to better understand their reality, and finally, the intervention of the bishops in the most important problems of the cities by pastoral letters and pronouncements.

In another section are listed "prophetic gestures" of support for the people such as "the explicit support of the hierarchy and the participation of pastoral agents in the struggles of the people for better conditions, salary, work, freedom of expression." Also "special stress must be given to the presence of the church among the workers" which up to now has been "insufficiently developed."

This part of the report opts for basic communities, in which the people discover "the force which comes from unity" while more traditional movements favour the middle class, and "it is more difficult for these movements to question the social life of their members and to bring about a conversion to the perspectives of the poor." (cf. Chapter 2).

In an interesting paragraph towards the end, the bishops give a picture of how they see their own role: "The urban pastoral demands the efficient discharge of the responsibilities of the bishop as an animator . . . working as a full and qualified assessor, in contact with the grass-roots, aiming to express in all its richness — and with all its tensions — the life and action of the local church."

Pastoral Planning Applied: Sao Paulo:

The huge sprawling city of Sao Paulo in the south of Brazil is not only the largest city in the country with some twelve million inhabitants, but is the largest of South America and the fastest growing city in the world. As such, it reflects, better than any other city, the urban problems which the CNBB Report analyses. And its pastoral activity in the light of these problems presents us with a very good example of how such pastoral planning is put into practice.

Cardinal Paulo Arns has been Sao Paulo's archbishop since 1970, and has a strong personal commitment to what he has called "Christian socialism". Consequently, as he put it to me, the diocese's "organic pastoral action is planned and elaborated on the basis of pastoral priorities, involving a greater participation of the people and leading the church to think of its activity as a service to the liberation of the people."

The current priorities of the archdiocese are set out in a colourful booklet called *What We, the Church in Sao Paulo, Are Going to Do*. This lists the four priorities which evolved from a series of meetings with elected representatives from the communities, parishes, sectors and regions of the church all over the city. These four priorities are completely in line with the CNBB plan: (1) basic communities; (2) human rights and the marginalized; (3) the world of work, and (4) the pastoral of the periphery. The booklet goes on: "This is the concrete form in which you can be the church today, as a participant in the activity and life of this church."

The booklet then gives concrete advice on what people can do to act on these priorities. It encourages them to get involved in local basic communities, or to begin one themselves, in order to overcome the main danger of city life "where people cannot be persons". On human rights and the marginalized it says: "Remaining passive, resigned, accepting injustice and discrimination, oppression and marginalization isn't in accordance with the Gospel of Christ." It recommends people to know the Universal Declaration of Human Rights and to make it known. When they see a human right violated, it encourages them to find, with their community, a concrete activity in defence of that right.

On 'The World of Work', the booklet tells workers that "Jesus Christ was a worker and depended on his companions to change this world." In the light of bad salaries and conditions, and a lack of any guarantee of work or of participation in the company, concrete recommendations are made: "Get to know the laws governing workers and find someone to explain them to you and your colleagues; join your trade union and take part in its meetings; arrange with your colleagues and form a workers' group in your local area." On the final priority, 'The People of the Periphery' people are recommmended to be involved in setting up community centres and basic communities, "to get those involved who have the skills to organize and animate so as to help the people to feel themselves more united." And for people "who don't suffer from the problems of the periphery, see that your community is organized in favour of the periphery of Sao Paulo."

The parish of Vila Alpina is a large suburban parish, predominantly lower middle class in composition and with some *favelas* or shanty town areas hidden among the simple but sturdy, brick-built houses. In order to apply the pastoral priorities of the archdiocese to their own needs, Vila Alpina held a parochial synod attended by Dom Luciano, the bishop of the local region, one of nine into which the archdiocese is divided, and more than seventy of the most active pastoral workers of the parish. Using the CNBB Pastoral Plan and the results of a questionnaire which had been distributed around the parish, the synod elaborated four pastoral priorities for the local needs: (1) human rights, the poor and marginalized; (2) the formation of leaders and ministers; (3) the pastoral of education, and (4) basic communities.

The numerous groups which are active in the parish reflect in different ways these priorities. The main activity of the twelve youth groups is making young people aware of poverty and exploitation and organizing activities to counteract it. While I was there, these groups had just collected thirty five thousand signatures for a petition to end torture. This practice, they said in their monthly youth magazine, showed government legislation to be "an affront to the most basic precepts of human dignity." The meeting of the co-ordinating team for all these youth groups which I attended was discussing how to do something to help the people of Nicaragua, then in the middle of their war against the Somoza dictatorship. They were also publicizing the issues of the metalworkers' strike which had just taken place, and which the government had declared to be illegal. A cartoon in their magazine clearly expressed the young peoples view: "It isn't the strike which is illegal, it is the salary the workers earn."

This metal-workers' strike had also been supported by the parish with statements at Masses, and with collections of food for the strikers' families. This had caused a debate at the Parochial Assembly because some parishioners disagreed. However, a majority committed the parish to "support workers' movements for better social conditions." As well as implementing their first priority in this way, parish workers were active in organizing the people in the *favelas*, some of whom were being threatened with forcible clearance. In this area, too, the parish was committed to "organizing the struggle of the people for better conditions."

The second parochial priority, the formation of leaders and ministers, I saw in action when I attended the ordination of a priest, who, as deacon, was in charge of a neighbouring parish, and the commissioning of a lay minister of marriage. While this was the first lay minister of marriage in Vila Alpina, the parish already has two lay ministers of baptism as well as six ministers for taking communion to the sick. These ministers, together with a team for celebrations and homilies, have taken over much of the liturgical work of the parish, thus freeing the priests for working more as co-ordinators of overall parish activity. The parish also has a Pastoral Council for Formation, responsible for running pastoral and theological courses to help people learn some skills which would allow them to become more active in parish work.

Priority number three is the pastoral of education, understood not only as religious training for children and young people but also as running courses for couples getting married and parents who want their children baptised. The parish has twenty three groups for marriage preparation who meet in the co-ordinators' homes for the diocese's compulsory courses before getting married. Similarly for baptism: the diocese refused to baptise children until at least one of the parents has attended a series of talks and discussions on parenthood. The religious training of children is entrusted to groups of parents who themselves come to meetings with one of the parish team of catechists, often members of the youth groups who do this in their spare time.

Vila Alpina's fourth priority is the development and support of basic communities. Already there are three well-organized communities in the parish, each of which has its own team of co-ordinators, and its own commissioned ministers of baptism and the liturgy. They organize their own activities, centred on the simple meeting place each has built or bought. The community also organizes its own liturgies every Sunday; and once a month one of the priests of the parish comes to celebrate the Eucharist with them.

The level of organization and popular involvement in Vila Alpina is high. It has become very actively a people's church, it runs most of its activities with no involvement by the three priests who are free to take on a role of more spiritual counselling as well as involvement in activities outside the parish. Fr Jorge Boran, the priest in charge, is both the Priest Coordinator of the Youth Pastoral for the whole archdiocese and the priest in charge of the Regional Council, a group made up mostly of lay people, who plan the activities of the region together with the regional bishop.

Despite this extensive organization and activity, Fr Jorge estimates that out of the fifty thousand people in the parish, at most only one thousand have any involvement with the church. But, then, this only serves to bear out what the CNBB plan so clearly said: "An effort which attends only to quantitative aspects will not be effective. What is essential is the quality of pastoral planning and its orientation."

Chile: The People Under Attack

The greatest challenge the Chilean Church has faced in recent times was undoubtedly the military coup of 11th September, 1973, which overthrew the democratically elected government of Salvador Allende. Instead of retreating into a safe haven of religious activities, the church immediately organized to defend the rights of the large number of people arbitrarily arrested. Already by 6th October, a mere twenty five days after the coup, the Committee for Peace was set up. Composed of an ecumenical board of directors with all the main Christian churches as well as the Jewish community represented, the committee set up two separate groups: one to defend the rights of the many foreigners who had come to live in Chile during the Allende period, many of them Marxists from Brazil, Argentina, and Paraguay and who were the target for government repression; the other group to defend the rights of Chilean people detained without trial by the military.

Fr Cristian Precht was executive secretary of this committee, and he told me of its early days: "The first months of the committee were spent mostly trying to help people live through an emergency: helping them with food, getting information about what was happening in the country and finding out where the disappeared people were." Then came the widespread military trials which took everyone by surprise as most had expected military rule to last only a few months before a return to democracy. "So then the church thought, we have to organize the defence of these people because nobody else dare defend the Marxists." With the spread of repression, union leaders began to be dismissed. So the committee took up their cases. "We knew we had to help the union leaders and to defend them juridically so that they could claim their rights and have their dismissals re-examined, because a lot of the time it was merely because of their political ideas that they had lost their jobs."

So the Committee for Peace grew from those faltering beginnings until it had a well organized structure. Different juridical services were provided: for those arrested, often without charge; for those dismissed from jobs, a group which became ever more numerous due to "the economic policy the government had and still have", as Fr Precht said; and a service to defend dismissed students and teachers. There was also a department co-ordinating programmes with the provinces and one whose main task was compiling information on disappeared persons. They also started social programmes in the shanty towns giving financial help to the organization of communal workshops to provide employment; and they were even forced to run food canteens to feed some of the estimated 30% of children who were hungry.

The committee was, however, meeting difficulties from two different sources. Firstly, some of the Protestant church leaders were coming under increasing pressure from their churches, which, because of their largely middle-class membership, were more in sympathy with the government. Bishop Helmut Frenz of the Chilean Luthern Church lost 75% of his church's membership when they set up their own church in protest at the bishop's support for the committee. Difficulties with the government came to a head in late 1975 after some priests and nuns had helped left-wing leaders escape from a military trap. President Pinochet wrote to Cardinal Silva asking him to disband the committee. At the same time sixteen collaborators of the committee, priests, nuns and lay people, were arrested, which, as Fr Precht puts it, "showed Pinochet was not begging but demanding".

After long discussion with the committee, it was agreeed that the Cardinal disband it but only to set a more effective organization. On the 1st January, 1976, he set up the Vicariate of Solidarity, appointing Fr Precht the episcopal vicar, who outlined to me the significance of this move: "We decided to create a vicariate, which is an official organization of the archdiocese, because the cardinal wanted to show his personal support for our work. By appointing me a vicar, who is the closest collaborator a bishop has, he was showing the continuity with what had been done in the past."

Drawing on what they had learned over the past two years, the vicariate was able to set up an elaborate structure with a full-time executive secretary, a layman, and six departments. Juridical Action deals with arrested people, trials and disappearances. The workers' department supports labour leaders and workers in their demands for just conditions and pay, and defends them when unjustly dismissed. The third department deals with supporting the work of solidarity in the eight pastoral zones of Santiago: food canteens, helping people organize to meet their problems, health programmes "helping the people to form a consciousness of being able to enforce their own right to health and to promote health care in their local area." The fourth department publishes a fortnightly bulletin, *Solidaridad*. The fifth maintains relations with dioceses all over the country, each of which has its own programmes of solidarity. The sixth department, called *Apoyo*, meaning Support, publishes information, guides to the people's rights and booklets dealing with the church's stand on various social questions. Most importantly it has published over six hundred detailed cases of disappeared persons in eight volumes, which were presented to the government and then made public. Again and again church leaders, from the cardinal down, keep demanding information from the government on where these people are and action in bringing those responsible to justice.

Such church work is constantly developing as is evidenced by the changes in the Vicariate of Solidarity. In 1977 its Workers' Department became a separate Workers' Vicariate. This was to concentrate on developing links with unions and on working in solidarity with them. The vicariate also takes any initiative it can to press home to the government the necessity of respecting people's rights. To mark Human Rights Year in 1978, they organized a major symposium in Santiago on the theme, "Every Human Being has the Right to be a Person." Leading churchmen from all over the world attended, as well as the director of the Human Rights division of the UN, the secretary general of Amnesty International and the secretary general of the International Commission of Jurists.

At public meetings youth leaders, workers' leaders and representatives of the families of the disappeared were able to voice their criticisms of the government. All the papers of this symposium were afterwards published in five well-produced volumes.

The fortnightly magazine, *Solidaridad*, is the vicariate's official voice, and one of the few truly free publications in present-day Chile. In issue after issue it highlights the people's falling living standards and articulates their aspirations against the dictatorship in a way the official press completely ignores. On May Day, though it reported the official government ceremony, it also reported the illegal march, the speeches made at it and the number of arrests. It openly criticises government actions, and is the only forum for discussing draft government legislation in an open, critical manner. In its reporting of international events such as the events in Nicaragua or El Salvador, it shows an example of the struggles of other peoples of Latin America against their dictatorships.

In an article to mark its third anniversary in June 1979, it criticised "the monopoly of information, as much on the part of governments as on the part of private interests, which permits the arbitrary use of the media of information and gives pride of place to sectional interests." It went on to criticise the "manipulation of information by transnational companies which ... spread cultural values, life-styles and models of development whose origin is in great measure based on a dominant transnational ideology."[1] The same article ends with a quotation from the Puebla conference summing up the magazine's own philosophy: "Knowing the situation of poverty, marginalization, and injustice in which large masses of Latin Americans are immersed, and also being aware of the violations of human rights, in its use of its own media the church must more and more each day become the voice of the dispossessed, even at the risk entailed." (par. 1094).

Cristian Precht thinks that the Vicariate of Solidarity has succeeded in making this more than a slogan: "Because we have people who really fight for human rights, understood both as personal and as social rights, we have become the voice of those who don't have a voice, even with all our limits and ambiguities." He goes on to speak of what he sees as being the effect of their work: "I am definitely sure that the action of the church during the past six years has stopped the repression being stronger and specifically has stopped the disappearances." But its significance is wider than that: "It has meant a rediscovery of the mission of the church for human rights and a new conscience for the church that it has to be a missionary church really trying to make an impact on the creativity of the society in which we are living."

In wider terms the Vicariate of Solidarity has been at the forefront of a process which has effected wide sectors of the Chilean Church since the coup. It was best summed up for me by Enrique Alvear, auxiliary bishop of Santiago: "The church was brought into contact with a world that it hadn't been in contact with before: the world of left-wing parties, a world more impregnated with the Marxist vision. This helped us all a lot because it served to show to those from this world of politics and Marxism a church preoccupied with man, without asking what his ideology was. And it helped the church to understand the thinking, the searching of this world. The church did this simply out of its commitment to the Gospel, to defend men and women and their human rights."

Panama: Research for Popular Needs

CEASPA, the Panamanian Centre for Studies and Social Action, is housed in a simple two storey house in the suburbs of Panama City. Set up by the Jesuits in 1977, it has five full-time researchers, economists and sociologists, together with four part-time associates. The then director of the Centre, Jesuit economist Xabier Gorostiaga, who has since become an economic advisor to the Nicaraguan government, described the team's basic commitment: "All we demand from those who want to co-operate with us in our work is that they have a clear class option for the peasants and workers." Their aim, far from being simply an academic research centre, is to "serve the integral development of the people within a pluralist and ecumenical conception of the popular church." The centre fulfills this role by background studies into topics such as "The Development of Capitalism in Panama 1840–1978," or "Transnational Companies and the Development of Agriculture in Latin America: The Case of Panama." Through these studies the team hope to make a contribution to the formation of policy in Panama in accordance with "the real needs of our people."

More practical programmes it has undertaken include a year's study of the pattern of infant nutrition in certain deprived areas of the city with the object of evolving practical educational programmes about nutrition. Another such practical study is on "Woman's Role in the Work Market of Panama." This study hopes to highlight areas distinctly relating to the oppression of women.

The centre provides a service to underprivileged groups to help them in their own activities by undertaking studies for them. It has done a study on uban social movements for some trade unions; and when I visited them they had just taken up the cause of the Guaymi Indians, whose traditional environment and means of livelihood are threatened by a huge copper mine complex which would make Panama one of the world's biggest copper producers.

This development, which will cost the Panamanian government £2.2 billion, has caused a national debate in the country. The left are backing the plan as it has potential greatly to help the development of the country. But CEASPA are the only group who have taken up the cause of the Indians. Xabier Gorostiaga explained the reasons for this to me: "It's not that we are against the mine. We agree with the Communist Party that it is the most important economic development ever to have taken place in Panama. But we take up the cause of the Guaymi Indians as a human cause, a Christian cause, not a political cause, because there's no political reason for doing it." As part of its campaign it has persuaded the episcopal conference to issue a pastoral letter on the topic, which CEASPA was preparing at the time.

CEASPA has close links with the Centro de Capacitacion Social who are a publishing house. They publish a monthly *Dialogo Social* which reflects the work of CEASPA, and has most of its researchers on its editorial board. *Dialogo Social* is now the major left-wing journal publishing serious analysis and comments on society and the economy in all the Central American countries. They also publish a series of little pamphlets for use in conscientisation work, called *Caminando*. Among titles already published are ones on the sacraments and popular religiosity, on Medellin and the preparation for Puebla, on human rights and 'Sovereignty in its Total Sense', on 'Work and Salaries' and on 'Who Does the Money Go To?'

These little booklets get their message across very effectively with comic drawings. The issue on the preparations for Puebla is a good example. This goes into "the scheming between the Puebla organizers and the traditionalists against the people and the popular church which the oppressed have forged in their struggles at the cost of many martyrs." The drawings illustrating the text show two workers talking over their drinks. They discuss the different types of bishops going to Puebla. Firstly the "traditionalists who only know how to say prayers and bless the clubs of the rich; they are authoritarian and they support fascist governments."[2] Illustrating this is a drawing of a bishop blessing troops with his diamond ring glistening on his finger. The second type are "developmentalists who are vacillators; they dress and speak in a modern way but they are afraid to be with the poor and they believe that development (roads, television, machines) will solve the problems of the people." Going with this is a drawing showing a 'trendy' young bishop standing smiling outside a modern church. Thirdly are the "progressives who are the most human and are decisively with the poor, living and working under the same persecution which Jesus Christ lived under; they don't believe only in development but in the total liberation of oppressed people, economically, culturally, spiritually." With this is a drawing showing a bishop standing at a barbed wire fence, which Uncle Sam is trying to break through, keeping him out. Around him stand poor men and women. And so the pamphlet goes on, helping to open the eyes of the people to the reality of the struggles within the church and society today.

While such outright criticism angers the bishops at times, CEASPA's relationship with the hierarchy goes through "highs and lows" as Xabier Gorostiaga said. Each group needs the other. The bishops depend on CEASPA to do background research and draft statements for them. And CEASPA needs the backing of the bishops to continue its important work unhindered. The ultimate aim for both is the service they provide to articulating and supporting the needs of the majority of the Panamanian people so usually forgotten in the process of development.

Chapter Five

THEOLOGIANS:
ARTICULATING THE PEOPLE'S FAITH

"Let two or three prophets speak and let the others weigh what is said."
1 Corinthians, 14:29

"The 'theology of liberation' is often connected (sometimes too exclusively) with Latin America; but it must be admitted that one of the great contemporary theologians, Hans Urs von Balthasar, is right when he demands a theology of liberation on a universal scale. Only the contexts are different, but the reality itself of the freedom 'for which Christ set us free' (cf Gal., 5:1) is universal. The task of theology is to find its real significance in the different concrete historical and contemporary contexts."
Pope John Paul II

What characterises the theology of liberation is that it is controversial. Not controversial for a small group of intellectuals, as is theology in the developed world, but of interest to the poor and oppressed. And because it is of interest to the poor and oppressed, so too is it of interest to the secret police of most Latin American countries, and of abiding and paranoid interest to the ruling class.

The almost universally hostile press coverage given to liberation theology throughout the Puebla Conference bears this out. Not alone did the press only too readily jump to the conclusion that the Pope was condemning the theology of liberation, but some newspapers waged campaigns against certain theologians, the most notable being the Puebla evening paper which ran a huge banner headline calling Gustavo Gutierrez a "liar."

The theology of liberation has also led secret service agents to take a renewed interest in theology. At the fourth Ecumenical Conference of Third World Theologians in Sao Paulo[1] (see below) the organisers avoided drawing up a list of participants in the fear that it might fall into the wrong hands; and internal security at the conference had to be very tight for the same reason.

But the hostile interest shown by the ruling class in the theology of liberation has been mirrored by an intensely positive interest in it

60

among the poor and oppressed, as is witnessed by the huge number of simple books, magazines, and typed-out sheets which circulate on theological themes among the basic Christian communities. Frei Betto, a leading Brazilian Dominican, who has himself been in prison for his beliefs, has observed that for the first time in centuries theology has come down out of rarefied atmosphere of lecture halls and become something discussed by ordinary people in pubs and cafes because it concerns their real lives.

This chapter tries to show both why and how the theology of liberation concerns the real lives of the oppressed of Latin America. The first part is a history of the background, beginning, and development of it. The second part describes some of its central ideas and how these are opposed to the liberal theology of the developed world. The final part is an introduction to, and an interview with, the man widely considered Latin America's greatest theologian at the moment, Leonardo Boff.

History

What is most surprising about the theology of liberation is that it exists at all. Though Latin America has been a predominantly Christian continent for centuries, it had never given rise to a distinctive theology, and had rested content with a second-rate imitation of European theology. This situation prevailed up into the sixties.

In Latin America, even more than in other parts of the world, the sixties was a decade of enormous change. While on the theological scene it was Vatican II which began the ferment, on the wider social and political scene it was the Cuban Revolution of January, 1959, which set the tone.

Vatican II's challenge was taken up enthusiastically by a group of young Latin American theologians. As early as March, 1964, a mere two years after the Council began, a group of these met at Petropolis in Brazil and pledged themselves to the search for the meaning of the Christian message in the context of the poverty and oppression of Latin America. Among those at the meeting were Gustavo Gutierrez and Juan Luis Segundo.

Wider events were already setting the agenda for this theological search. The sixties were the 'Decade of progress' for the US in Latin America; but more profound forces than US policy were changing the continent. In the military takeover in Brazil in 1964 was to be seen the response of an oligarchy increasingly feeling under threat from the rising ferment of revolutionary ideas. President Johnson's haste to congratulate the country's new military rulers showed the true nature of US interest in the continent.

The imagination of the young was caught by the symbolic example of Che Guevara naively trying to export the Cuban experience to the mountains of Bolivia. But, for Christians, far more symbolic was the example of the Colombian priest, lecturer in sociology and chaplain at the National University of Bogota, Camilo Torres.

As early as 1964 Torres had reached his conclusions. A long paper he gave to an international symposium in Louvain, Belgium, in September of that year, was entitled simply "Revolution: Christian Imperative". The following year this led him to apply for laicisation, not in order to give up his priesthood but in order to live it out as an active guerrilla.

"I have given up the duties and privileges of the clergy, but I have not ceased to be a priest," he said in a message to Christians. "I believe that I have given myself to the revolution out of love for my fellow man. I have ceased to say Mass to practise love for my fellow man in the temporal, economic and social spheres. When my fellow man has nothing against me, when he has carried out the revolution, then I will return to offering Mass, God permitting."[2] Camilo Torres was shot dead by Government troops in the mountains of Colombia on February 15th, 1966.

Other Christians too were taking up the same concerns as Camilo Torres. By 1966, these were grouping themselves in basic Christian communities in Chile and Brazil, supporting one another in their new understanding of the radical demands of Christian faith for political struggle. It was this new practice of the faith which provided much of the impetus for the young theologians of the continent.

This new understanding found its first clear and authoritative expression in the Medellin conference in 1968, whose conclusions themselves both served to legitimise the new movement and to strengthen it all over the continent. Liberation theology had established itself.

The new theology found its definitive expression as well as its definitive name three years later when the Peruvian theologian, Gustavo Gutierrez, published his systematic and wonderfully comprehensive book called simply *A Theology of Liberation*. In his introduction to the book, Fr Gutierrez describes it as "an attempt to describe and interpret the forms under which the Latin American Church is present in the process of liberation — especially among the most committed Christtian groups — [which] will allow us to establish the questions for an authentic theological reflection."[3] And he goes on to make it clear that he isn't dealing with themes which are of interest only to Latin Americans, or peripheral to Christian faith: "The question regarding the theological meaning of liberation is, in truth, a question *about the very meaning of Christianity and about the mission of the Church.'*[4]

Not only did Gutierrez's book lay the definitive groundwork for the new theology, establishing it as genuine theology drawn both from Scripture and the tradition of the Church, but it also posed a question and a challenge for all other theology which regards itself as Christian.

The ground was now ready for a rich and ever diversified stream of theological writing from all over Latin America. Already in 1971 was published *Marx and the Bible* by the Mexican Jesuit, Jose Miranda, a book which in some ways can be said to pre-date liberation theology as such. Miranda uses the latest discoveries of biblical scholarship to establish, through detailed analysis of certain texts of Scripture, the simple but revolutionary conclusion that "the biblical authors implacably insist that a god who is conceived as existing outside the interhuman summons to justice and love is not the God who revealed himself to them, but rather some idol . . . God will only be in a world of justice, and if Marx does not find him in the Western world it is because he is indeed not there, nor can he be."[5]

In 1971 the Uruguayan Jesuit, Juan Luis Segundo, also published his five-volume series called *Theology for the Artisans of a New Humanity*. This series illustrates the method of liberation theology very clearly. The series grew out of courses for adults on the basic themes of theology — church, grace, God, sacraments, redemption — but not to "spell out all the avatars of a doctrine laden with the accumulations of twenty centuries." Rather its aim was to situate it "on the level of the Christian's real-life questions."[6] Each volume therefore includes the introductory talk of each course session but also a series of "clarifications" based on the questions raised by the participants and a section of quotations from the Bible and from Vatican II.

While the result of Segundo's approach is fresh and inspiring, and illustrates well the concern of liberation theologians to base their reflections on the questions and faith experience of people today, its questions have now been superceded by the developing political practice of Latin American Christians. It remains a useful index of just how far liberation theology has travelled in a short space of time.

Segundo followed this early work with a book entitled *The Liberation of Theology* in 1975. This is an examination of the methodology of the new theology, its relationship to sociology, to political options, and to ideology. As the title indicates, Segundo views the new methods and perspectives of the theology of liberation as themselves leading theology back to its true function. His conclusion is that "the pathways opened up here lead into a long and unforeseeable future."[7]

This has been more than verified already in the remarkable diversity and richness of themes that theologians of liberation have taken up. The Chilean theologian, Segundo Galilea, unfortunately little known in the English-speaking world, has made his own the theme of the popular culture of the oppressed and the spirituality which their struggles for liberation have given birth to. One of his early books, published in 1973, is called *Spirituality of Liberation.*

Leonardo Boff published his first book, *The Gospel of the Cosmic Christ* in 1971, but it is for his second book, *Jesus Christ Liberator* that he has become best known. Boff's overriding interest is in the person of Jesus and his message. "The revolutionary message of Christ had been reduced to a decision of faith made by individuals without relation to the social and historical world, their natural context," he says in *Jesus Christ Liberator.* "The message had been preached with the use of categories taken from the context of intimate, private, I-Thou, interpersonal relationships. Conversion too had taken on a private character and had come to mean a change in the life of an individual, not calling for any involvement in the politico-social world that remained safeguarded against all criticism."[8]

Following Boff in his concern to rescue the true message of Jesus from the limited and one-sided way it has been understood by much of modern theology is the young Jesuit from El Salvador, Jon Sobrino. His much acclaimed work *Christology at the Crossroads: A Latin American Approach*, published in 1976, was an attempt to move from the position of European theology which tries to explain Christ in rational terms to a position of demonstrating the message of Christ from its capacity to subvert the present way society is organised and lead to the Kingdom of justice, peace and love.

Yet another concern is that of the relationship of the Church to political struggles, a concern taken up by Ignacio Ellacuria, also from El Salvador, in his book *Freedom Made Flesh: The Mission of Christ and his Church,* published in Spanish in 1973. In Brazil a brother of Leonardo Boff, Clodovis Boff, has taken up the same theme in a book entitled *Ecclesial Community, Political Community* not yet translated into English.

Enrique Dussel, an Argentinian layman, is the leading historian within the liberation theology perspective; and he has published a history of the Latin American Church called *Colony and Liberation (1492-1972).*

Jose Comblin, a Belgian who was expelled from Brazil for his work with Helder Camara, now works in Talca in Chile and has published studies on he ideology of National Security and the relationship of the church to the military regimes of the continent.

Neither is the theology of liberation an exclusively Catholic pursuit. Protestant theologians like Rubem Alves, Julio de Santa Ana, and, particularly, Jose Miguez Bonino, have successfully established a liberation theology approach within Protestant theology and share the same concerns and outlook as their Catholic counterparts. To this extent it can be said that the theology of liberation is a post-ecumenical theology in that the traditional divisions of Catholic/Protestant hold little importance for it.

A sign of the maturity of liberation theology is that, though it began as a response to a Latin American situation, its influence has spread far outside the continent. The most notable effect it has had is in the grouping of Third World theologians representing Asia, Africa, the West Indes as well as Latin America. They held their fourth ecumenical conference in Sao Paulo, Brazil, from 20th February to 2nd March, 1980.

What is significant about this grouping is the genuine criticism, one of the other, that takes place within it, but always from within the basic perspective of concern for the liberation of the oppressed. At the Sao Paulo conference the Latin Americans met some criticism from their Asian and African counterparts for reducing such issues as racism and the oppression of women to the issue of class oppression. All agreed, however, that these issues can only be solved within the struggle for socialism.

The Sao Paulo conference also symbolised vividly the political commitment of liberation theologians, as it celebrated the liberation of Nicaragua and of Zimbabwe, and the Grenada revolution. Daniel Ortega of the Nicaraguan government addressed the conference, emphasising that political liberation can cause even greater economic isolation and thus suffering, for a people. Significantly, too, the relationship of political liberation to the Kingdom was one of the major theological issues taken up. The final document stated that the Kingdom of God is foreshadowed and manifested in particular historical liberations such as in Nicaragua and Grenada, but is not to be identified with them.

Ultimately, what contrasts the theology of liberation most with the liberal theology of the West is its sheer vigour and output. Having broken out of the immunised world of academia, and having rooted itself firmly among the oppressed, the theology itself has taken on the urgency and vigour of the struggles of the oppressed. Theology has become something real once again.

Content

The theology of liberation begins with and is defined by the discovery of Christ in the poor. Leonardo Boff in an interview given at Puebla spoke for all liberation theologians in describing this discovery: "The seminary gives us an academic formation based on theory. We must realise this, get out of the centre of the city where the big religious houses are, and go into the slums and feel there the tremendous impact on our consciousness. Only to the extent that we take this consciousness seriously will our lives be changed."

This discovery of the poor forces a radical re-evaluation of the traditional concepts and priorities of Christian faith from the standpoint of the struggles of the poor for liberation. For Gustavo Gutierrez: "The roots of the theology of liberation lie in the process of the people's struggles, in their living faith, in the experiences of the following of Jesus in the context of the defence of the rights of the poor, and the preaching of the Gospel amid the struggles for liberation. This is its world. Because of this, the theology of liberation is much more attentive to what is happening in this world than to the observations and criticisms of the academic world, no matter how valid these may be."[9]

What is new about this theology then is not so much in its content as in its method: theology in many parts of the world increasingly takes up political themes and uses much of the terminology of liberation theology. But, in Segundo's telling phrase, until it is "more interested in being liberative than in talking about liberation"[10] it is not liberation theology.

Reflecting on Christian faith from the standpoint of the oppressed has led liberation theologians to be critical of the naivety of the prevailing liberal theology of the developed world which does not realise just how much its own starting point is conditioned by its social position. Gustavo Gutierrez expresses this in one very hard-hitting passage: "Their universe is that of modern society and bourgeois ideology. The point of departure for the theology of liberation is not only different from that of liberal theology but it is in fact in historical contradiction with it. This is a contradiction which has its roots in social reality. The dialectical opposition to bourgeois ideology and the dominant culture comes from the popular classes.

"The exploited social classes, the despised races, the marginalised cultures, those whom we don't know intimately in their vitality and energy but can only look in upon, as it were, from the outside, those whom the Bible calls the poor, they are the historical subject of this new understanding of the faith."[11]

The contrasts, therefore, are sharp. They pervade the whole process and content of theology. Breaking out of the abstractions of both pre- and post-Vatican II theology, liberation theologians have begun to discover again the perspectives and priorities of the biblical message.

In rediscovering the Bible as the history of an oppressed people and of their hope for liberation, the theology of liberation has also rediscovered the God of the Bible. "It is necessary to remember that the God of the Bible is not just a God who governs history," says Gustavo Gutierrez, "but he orients history towards the establishment of justice and of right. He is more than a provident God. He is a God who takes the side of his people and who liberates them from slavery and oppression."[12]

The true God, therefore, can only be known in the struggle for justice and peace. This is the clear and unequivocal teaching of the

Bible, so clear in fact that Gustavo Gutierrez can say: "In the liberation of the poor is given the true 'theophany', the revelation of God."[13]

Rediscovering God means rediscovering the thrust of Jesus' message. Jesus didn't come to preach himself, rather he came to preach the Kingdom of God, the reign of justice and liberation which will be established by the poor, the oppressed, the marginalised of history.

The call of God, therefore, is the call to conversion to the standpoint of the poor, the call to side with them historically in their struggles. "To know and love God it is necessary to know the social conditions of the poor today and to transform radically the society which creates these conditions,"[14] says Gustavo Gutierrez. It is in answering this call that the church is born, the *ecclesia* or assembly of those who make their own the practice of Jesus, and, through it, live out the new social relationships of fraternity which are the sign of the coming liberation of the oppressed.

The church, for the liberation theologians, is the network of those Christian communities who are struggling within the historical social conditions of today for a radically new type of society. It is to be found in that network of basic communities all over the Latin American continent, communities which are, as it were, the seeds of a new society.

In breaking down the traditional hierarchical model of the church, liberation theology has also broken down the division between evangelisers and evangelised, subject and object. Indeed, theologians and bishops frequently state that they have learned the Gospel from the poor, and realise that it is only by staying close to the poor that they can continue to live the Gospel.

Gone, therefore, is a band of professionals, the clergy, who knew the message, preaching to those who did not, the laity. The learning process now becomes two-way with theologians and clergy listening to the oppressed and learning from them, and then providing the means for the poor, in their communities, to learn more of the skills that can help them in their own liberation.

It is for this reason that the liberation theologians criticise their European and North American counterparts for the luxury of their concerns, namely preaching the Gospel to the non-believer. In Latin America the concern rather has become how to preach the Gospel to the non-man, to the person who hasn't enough to live on.

Taking the non-man seriously means rediscovering what love is all about. This is the concrete love as Jesus practised it, confronting the oppressor and finally being killed by that same oppressor. "To sin, not to love, not to know God, is to create relations of injustice, is to opt for oppression and against liberation,"[15] Gustavo Gutierrez reminds us.

Such love must be based on hope, a hope·that liberation is possible, a hope that history will lead to liberation. For the oppressed this hope is vital, but it is also a hope which is central to the message of the Bible which promises liberation. This hope is based on a faith in the true God who guided the people of Israel to their liberation, a faith that he still guides the oppressed in their struggles for liberation. The traditional values of faith, hope, and love are then rediscovered in their true meaning.

In this sense, liberation theology is nothing new. It is older and more traditional than any other theology because it has taken the perennial themes of Christian theology and rediscovered their rich and vital meaning. For liberation theologians the real test that theirs is a valid interpretation of the Christian message is that they are persecuted for their theology. At times they feel they need to remind the theologians in the developed world that so too were Jesus and the apostles.

Leonardo Boff: A View from Inside

When the 42 year-old Brazilian Franciscan priest, Leonardo Boff, published his best known book, *Jesus Christ Liberator* in English in 1978, he added a final chapter which he says in his preface could not be written when the book was first published in 1972 because "it was being put together at a time when severe political repression was being exerted against broad segments of the church."[16]

This is both a comment on the commitment of Leonardo Boff, widely recognised as Latin America's leading theologian, and also a comment on the commitment of liberation theology as a whole. It is a theology reflecting on and articulating the critical faith of the oppressed of the continent; a theology committed to radical social and political change.

But liberation theology finds itself under attack from another quarter. A sign of this is that, though Leonardo Boff is in much demand as a writer and speaker all over Latin America and beyond, he is forbidden to preach in his own diocese because of his views. It is for some of these views that his work has been under review by the Vatican's Sacred Congregation for the Doctrine of the Faith since *Jesus Christ Liberator* was published.

This examination is still continuing in 1980 but it is another sign of the Latin American church that a controversial theologian has vigorous episcopal defenders in the persons of two of Brazil's leading cardinals, both of them Franciscans, Cardinals Lorscheider and Arns. Cardinal Arns, who taught Fr Boff theology, has discussed his case in Rome and pointedly promised: "Boff will not be punished," adding: "It is hard to understand how Rome can treat people like this."

His examination has not stopped Leonardo Boff from writing. Since his first book in 1971 he has written twenty four more, and also edits Brazil's top religious journal *Revista Eclesiastica Brasileira* as well as being Portuguese editor of the prestigious international theological journal *Concilium.*

I met him in the small town of Petropolis in the cool of the hills outside Rio, where he teaches theology in the Franciscan Theological Seminary, and is the chief religious editor for Editora Vozes, a publishing house owned by the Franciscans.

In a small front room of the community house where he lives, he spoke with evident feeling and commitment about the Church but showed nothing of the reserve usually associated with academics. What struck me about Leonardo Boff were his penetrating brown eyes, an indication of the firm commitment that came through as he spoke.

Q: What have been the most important developments in the Latin American Church?

Leonardo Boff: I believe that the advances aren't primarily theological but pastoral. This signifies that there is the priority of the practice of the church over the reflection of the church. The church in these last years, since Vatican II, but in a much more decisive manner since Medellin, has defined its new social position within Latin American reality. It's a Church which wants to incarnate itself, preferentially though not exclusively, among the exploited classes in the poor areas, and from the standpoint of the poor to redefine its function within history and its relationship to other social classes.

This new position of the church within historical society changes the stress of its message and of the way it lives. This new stress is to articulate an evangelisation with justice, an evangelisation with human rights, with social development, with liberation. And especially it is a prophetic church which denounces the oppression of the great majority and which wants to be a force for social change. I think this is what characterises the practice of the church. And from this basis begins the reflection which tries to get to the roots of theology from within this practice of the faith, to illuminate it and to give it a stronger consistency and efficiency.

Q: What consequences can you see for this process?

L B: There are two great consequences of this. One is the creation of a new type of church, not a new church, but a new way of the church being present; a church not defined by a clericalism due to ordination and sacraments etc. but a church much more the People of God, a great web of communities with a new style of distribution of power, with a new style of being priest, of being bishop, with a re-definition of the functions of religious life. I believe strongly in this creation of a new type of church.

And the second consequence is that it will be a church much more committed to change in society, and will be one of the forces for this change. Traditional sociological analysis based on thinkers like Karl Marx, Max Weber and others assert that religion plays a conserving social role, legitimising established power and justifying the ruling classes in their domination. I believe we now have a new realisation that Christianity isn't a confirmation of the status quo; but more and more it makes itself a force for change. For this it is a church that must be very vigilant, which knows in different countries the open repression which exists; and the price of this recognition is a commitment to those classes interested in change which are the marginalised and oppressed classes.

So I believe we see a new type of church, and this is a factor in the birth of a new type of society especially one involving the participation of the popular classes. I believe this development will grow ever stronger.

Q: What do you think is the specific Christian contribution to social change?

L B: It is time now to say clearly that Christianity with its most distinctive ideals from its founding texts, the great tradition of Scripture, is much closer to socialism than it is to capitalism; and that there is a sort of co-naturality. I belive that the socialism which is being built up in Latin America will be one with social forms allowing more participation. This will come out of the present crisis and will have the Christian tradition as one of its great inspirations.

I don't believe in a Christian socialism, but I do believe in a socialism within which it will be much easier for Christians to live their Christian ideals. For this reason I believe Christians will work for a more humanitarian, a more participatory, a more democratic socialism, with less inequality. This is what is happening especially in the basic communities: these are new democratic forms, they are new forms of participation. The more this develops, the more are Christians active in changing society. And it postulates a more socialised form of society. But this is a long process because the contradictions are very strong and the repression is very powerful.

Q: There is much criticism in the Brazilian Church of the conservative pressure of Rome. What is your opinion?

L B: I believe there is a real plot between some bishops, along with Cardinal Baggio in the Vatican and the president of CELAM, Archbishop Lopez Trujillo, to perpetuate an old model of the church, centralised and Romanised, especially Romanised. I believe this plot goes against affirming the particular church, against the creation of a church which is more the People of God, more decentralised. One can understand this from within a dialectical process in which the old forces who feel themselves still effective, though less so than before, react with all the power they have. But the church born of the faith of the people is strong because there are committed bishops, archbishops and cardinals who believe in this church and who can't be kept quiet. But we have to watch with vigilance not only against the forces of political repression but also against the forces of ecclesiastical repression.

I believe that the alliance against this among the church born of the people is being better articulated all the time with examples of people in positions of leadership, bishops, archbishops and cardinals, who have understood the evangelical greatness of this church and, who can defend this little flower more and more. We must be very clear in understanding this plot which has its own strategy, its means of naming and transferring bishops, of defaming others and of putting pressure directly on theologians and bishops. It must be denounced at an international level as a real plot which has names such as Baggio and Lopez Trujillo. This is my clear position.

Q: How do you think Christians in the developed world regard the theology of liberation?

L B: The signs are that ever more Christians, and among them priests and bishops, are accompanying our church with a lot of interest, whether it is our pastoral experiences or whether it is the theology which is being done here. They see it as a privileged situation of a new incarnation of the faith within another culture which is the culture of the poor; not a different culture but the culture of another class, the culture of silence, of poverty, the popular culture. A church which is incarnating itself in this culture is indeed incarnating itself in another continent, in another cultural universe. I believe that ever more people understand this and support it.

For me a great sign of hope is that in Europe they want to learn, because up to now they have taught us, the theologians. I personally studied five years in Germany, and now to our surpirse we see them as a church, theologians, bishops, who want to learn. This I believe is very important. This is something of the Spirit, not egoism.

Chapter Six

MISSIONARIES:
SERVING THE POPULAR NEEDS

"The Spirit of the Lord is upon me, because he has anointed me to preach good news to the poor. He has sent me to proclaim release to the captives and recovery of sight to the blind, to set at liberty those that are oppressed."

Luke 4:18

"The Church has the duty to proclaim the liberation of millions of human beings, many of whom are her own children — the duty of assisting the birth of this liberation, of giving witness to it, of ensuring that it is complete."

Pope Paul VI in Evangelii Nuntiandi

The Latin American church has always depended on priests and nuns from the United States, Canada and Europe, and still does to this day. In some countries foreigners make up a majority of the clergy, and thus have a large influence on church policies and direction. But, if in the past missionaries have been criticised for imposing foreign models of the church little adapted to the local needs, today foreign church workers are often among the most committed to the poor in their struggles.

The three examples that make up this chapter come from very different parts of the continent and very different situations, the suburbs of Mexico City, rural Bolivia, and the inner city of Recife in the northeast of Brazil. Yet they all serve to illustrate a common experience of foreigners working in the church in Latin America today who stress that it is through working among the poor that they have really begun to learn the true meaning of the Gospel.

Tlalnepantla: Insecure for the People

At home in Ireland, he is known as Jimmy, but in Mexico City he is Jaime (pronounced High-me). Jaime Fogarty has been a priest now for

73

twenty-five years, and for him it is the only life where he can satisfy his restlessness.

It is hard to know where to begin with him. As he drove me out to the poor *colonia* (shanty town) of Tlalnepantla on the very outskirts of Mexico City, where he has been pastor for the last two years, Jaime was talking about the rural co-operative in the state of Zacatechas, about six hours' drive north of Mexico City. For eighteen months he had worked hard at founding the cooperative. "If I'd have known all the pre-paratory work it would take I'd probably never have started," he admitted frankly. He has managed at this stage to get a grant of £40,000 which has enabled them to irrigate land which up to now could never be used. "But it's great soil when it is properly irrigated; and the people are now growing three crops a year in it." So far they have involved thirty families. "They each pay a minimum of 2,000 pesos (about £50) and for that they have a share in the land. It's too early yet to see returns on this money, but all our forecasts are that they should make a living from it." Jaime stressed strongly how in-debted he was to aid agencies: "Without money from home we just couldn't have begun."

But, in spite of all his hard work for the cooperative, it is not his main involvement. It is the five thousand people of the Colonia Isidro Febella in Tlalnepantla are Jaime's people. Situated on a dusty hillside at least an hour from the centre of Mexico City, the *colonia* houses the poorest of the poor. "All of these have moved in from the countryside in the last thirty years looking for work; they just move in and put up some sort of shelter and stay. Over the years they might get some money and build a small brick house, but many don't even get that far." After we turned off the main road, we were in a jumble of corrugated iron shacks, some tiny brick houses and some which were only a bit of canvas over a few poles. Between these ran unpaved, dusty streets. The children ran up to the car to say Hallo to the *padre;* one group sang a song for us. Everywhere people had a friendly greeting. Jaime was obviously known and appreciated. "Before I came, there was no priest would stay here," Jaime told me as we climbed up to the starkly simple church with its view out over the colonia. "If the people wanted Mass they put some money together and went to a priest with it — it was a business deal. There were maybe twenty or thirty people coming to Mass when I came here, now we have about three hundred."

Jaime's way of doing things is by example. "Even if I had a million pounds, I wouldn't give them money. That's what the Americans do, they think they can solve problems that way. The important thing is to make them more self-aware, to make them see they can improve their own colonia. So on one of the first Sundays, I flung off my vestments after Mass and began mixing cement outside the church.

Some men joined in and even some of the old women helped, carrying water. The next Sunday a few more men turned up. It was the first time they saw a priest who would get his hands dirty and who would drink a beer or a tequilla (the local spirits) with them in their houses." This way, they put windows and doors in the church, built an annex on to it, and laid steps half way up the hillside to it. "The most important thing isn't the building but showing them it's possible to work together and get things done."

Since then, Jaime has started a co-operative for the women in the annex of the church, again with Irish money. "Trocaire [the Irish Catholic Church Agency for World Development] gave us £3,000 to buy machines and material, and I have a group of nuns who come out from the city to teach handcrafts every Monday." He has set up a dispensary in three rooms they rented in the area. He got some medical students and a nurse who helped; and the local municipality paid for the medicines. "I have organised it independently of the church so that it won't be in danger of being discontinued after I might go," Jaime told me. "The people elect a committee who run it." He set up a credit union for the people to try to give them the habit of saving. "The problem with them is that, when they have money, they spend it. They have no idea of saving." He has got a team of eight catechists together, girls from the colonia, who teach about three hundred children in the church every Saturday. He also has a Legion of Mary group who do some visitation.

Jaime has few illusions about his work. "I'm not the political type, I don't think about organising revolutions, though I think one is necessary here. I leave that to others. I try to do a few things with the people to help make life a little better. I know it's not much but it's something." One of the small facts he counts as a success is that the local municipality has chosen the man who works closest with Jaime to be leader of the colonia. "He told me he wanted to continue working with the church, but I said to him that was what the church was for — to help the colonia and that we would help him in every way we could."

As well as all this, Jaime edits the local diocesan paper, the *Gaceta Oficial* and works a little with the organisation of Chicano (Mexican American) priests, of which he is the only non-Chicano member.

How did a Tipperary man end up among the poorest of the poor in Latin America? Jaime joined the diocese of Salt Lake City, Utah, after his studies in Ireland. After seventeen years there, he had got working with the Chicanos and was involved in financing a girl from his parish to work in Latin America. "So seven years ago I asked the bishop if I could go to Mexico for a year to learn Spanish. He gave me the go-ahead; and, when here, I got more and more involved in working with the people, so I've stayed. I gave up a lot of security to come here;

it's not like a religious order, where you know you can fall back on the order. In Mexico there are no pension funds or sickness funds for priests — they just have to make do with what they get. Some do very well for themselves but I know some who are almost destitute." But Jaime has not regretted it. "When I get back to Salt Lake City, I see all the priests are interested in is a new carpet in the church, or becoming a monsignor, or something like that. At a certain stage in your life, you need a new challenge. I've found it here. But it wasn't easy. For the first time in my life I felt the pinch." So much did he feel that pinch, that he went to work as a teacher for two years in a state school to earn enough money to live on. After he gave that up, he was thinking of getting into journalism and he started a course, but gave it up after one term. "I always meant to go back, but there just seems to be so much else to do. Then I got involved in this co-operative and it took so much time."

Jaime is a man full of ideas and schemes, and full of the restless energy to carry them out. But underlying all this is a basic, down-to-earth concern for the poor and their problems which keeps him involved with them. "I could easily go full time into the co-operative, but then what would happen to the people of the colonia? Every time I bring an Irish person around, the rumour starts that I'm being taken home and I have to re-assure them I'm staying."

Also important to Jaime is his independence. "The bishop doesn't know half of what I'm doing; he's just glad there's a priest in the colonia. It's better that way. If I had to go through the bishop's office for my co-operative, I'd never have got it off the ground. He'd have insisted on taking some of the money for a seminary or a church or something like that. That's the mistake the Americans made in the sixties — they gave the money to the bishops, but none of it was used for social projects. It went in the seminary or the cathedral."

Jaime Fogarty might go under the Spanish form of his name but that's about all the Mexicans have managed to change. He's Irish through and through. "The curate in Thurles told me once that it was lucky all the restless guys like me went abroad — it meant they could live in peace in Ireland!" It's certainly lucky for the people of Tlalnepantla that Jimmy Fogarty went abroad, and they do not have to be told that.

Coroico: Accused of Being Communists

Coroico is a small town just sixty miles north of La Paz, Bolivia, but the fastest drive there takes four hours and in the wet season can take over a day. The road, said to be one of the ten most spectacular roads in the world, winds from La Paz to a height of over fifteen thousand feet and then falls to five thousand, clinging to a rock face with a sheer drop into a lush green valley thousands of feet below. If there is cloud clinging to the mountains, you drive right up through the cloud emerging into the clear sunlight beyond, and looking down on a sea of white filling in the valley below.

This is the road that the four sisters in Coroico, three Irish and one Irish-American, have got used to travelling in all weathers. Sometimes they have had to spend the night on the road when, as often happens in the rainy season, the road is blocked both in front and behind them. Sr Justin and Sr Margarite have been in Coroica about nine years; and Chris and Ceil joined them just over a year ago. They belong to the Franciscan Sisters of the Immaculate Conception. Coroico itself, where they have their house, is a small town whose population has dropped from five thousand to under two thousand in the last twenty years, but it is the capital of the province and the seat of the bishop. The area, Justin described to me as "the size of Ireland", and the part of it the sisters try to cover is "as big as any Irish county."

But even describing the size in this way gives no idea of the difficulties of getting around it. In the tropical foothills of the Andes, it is a succession of hills and valleys with little communities dotted everywhere. The roads are the worst imaginable. In the dry season they are at least hard mud; but the most potholed boreen in Ireland is a highway compared to them, with bumps and holes the rule rather than the exception. In the wet season I cannot imagine the quagmire the roads must become. This means that the sisters are out on the road literally every day from March to October because some of the communities can be cut off for weeks or even months in the rainy season.

The population is mostly native Indian, speaking their own languages, Quechua and Aymara. The townspeople are mostly descended from Spanish stock who intermarried with the Indians; and Coroico presents the unique feature of having a black population, brought in by the Spaniards as an experiment which failed to work. The truth of this small backward world is brutal to those who can so easily romanticise the simple ways of the peasant. The townspeople look down on the Quechua speakers, who look down on the Aymara speakers, who in turn look down on the blacks, as Chris told me.

The sisters work almost exclusively with the country people because they are the ones most exploited by their own and forgotten about by the government. The situation of these country people is very bad. The sisters estimate that the illiteracy rate is over 60%. Most mothers are quite willing to allow their child to die, as long as it is baptised; and they show no sorrow. They are suspicious of medicine and will accuse a doctor or nurse of killing a person who dies after treatment.

Economically, they are completely exploited by their own. Their main income comes from coffee and citrus fruits, mainly oranges and bananas, but they sell these to people in the town who own a lorry to bring the crop to La Paz, at very low prices. When I asked some of these *campesinos* (poor farmers) why they did not take their crops to La Paz themselves, they said they had tried, but found they were not allowed to sell them there. There is an unwritten monopoly controlled by five large families in the capital who export coffee to the US and Europe; they will only take the coffee from the buyers in the towns who keep the price low by keeping the growers dependent on them. One American economist who has studied the situation said that, with the control each of these families has, "You could be a millionaire in a year."

With people in La Paz making millions out of the coffee crop, the growers have to live on about £150 a year, an income which has not risen for years. Meanwhile, prices have been shooting up in Bolivia. Sugar prices, for example, have doubled; and tools are getting more expensive. All this is happening while the price of coffee has been going up on the world market, but these growers will never see any of this.

The great fear of the ruling class in this situation is to see the campesinos organised and educated. So this is exactly what the sisters saw they had to do. The first small scheme was a programme, set up by Margarite, to teach the women home skills. They persuaded each community to pick two young women they could spare during November, a month when the campesinos are not very busy. The sisters brought them into their own house, and organised a course in such things as hygiene, making clothes, nutrition, and skills useful for the women of the community. The idea was that they go home and hand on what they had learned to the other women. To implement this takes a lot of hard work and persuading. "They promise they'll come," said Margarite, "but when the day comes for enrollment, almost no one turns up." Yet, in spite of all their setbacks, they did manage to get people along, and the courses have been running quite successfully for the last few years.

This experience got the sisters accepted as being genuinely on the side of the campesinos. Out of it they were able to develop local leadership in each of the communities they visit. The leaders take on many of the functions of the priest for these communities, some of which see a priest only once a year. They hold prayer services every Sunday, teach the people their faith, organise the community to support sick members and families in particular need. They try to get the people to better themselves in whatever ways they can. The one hundred and fifty or so catechists, as they are called, have regular meetings in the sisters' house to discuss their needs, advance their education, and share their experiences. When I was in Coroico, there was a group of thirty catechists in for the week on such a meeting, completely organised and run by themselves. They were of Indian stock, Aymara speakers, in their late twenties and thirties mostly, all but five men. I spent an hour with them one morning discussing their work and situation. Never before have Indian people had such an opportunity to organise and improve themselves as this gives them and their communities. They spoke to me a lot about their exploitation at the hands of the townspeople and the politicians, and even asked me for advice as to who they should vote for in the coming elections. They are used to being promised the earth by politicians only to be forgotten after the elections. For them religion is very much applied to their real situation. One of them told me that to be Christian today they must be political, committed to the unions, to changing the political and economic situation of the country. Another used Christ's advice to unite in an openly political sense. Unite and organise to overcome their exploitation. That morning they sang too in Aymara, a hearty singing, and they prayed in the open spontaneous way in which they lead their communities in prayer. For them and their communities, this is an experience of re-finding a dignity for centuries denied by both church and state, an affirmation of their culture and distinctiveness that, once experienced, will be much more difficult to repress again.

Another more recent programme Chris and Ceil have started is called CETHA, the Centre for Technological, Humanistic and Agricultural Education. A team of five young local teachers and the two sisters visit five centres each week, teaching the adults basic literacy skills, maths, and what we would call civics, something about their society and history. At the moment they are on an experimental four year programme which they devise themselves and evaluate regularly, and are catering for about two hundred and seventy adult students. The level is, of course, very basic, but the students in the centre in Cruz Loma, about a half hour outside Coroico which I visited with the team, were very enthusiastic about what it is doing for them. The team hope to progress to a stage which could concentrate more on the roots of injustice in their society.

Near Coroico in Carmen Pantha an American brother, Nilus, who runs a primary and secondary school on his own, is experimenting with improving the coffee crop. He has begun a co-operative which cuts out the middle-man and is able to give the campesinos a third more for their crop of coffee than they could otherwise get. The day I visited the village, Brother Nilus was in a bulldozer building a bridge to link up a road opening up more villages. Sister Justin hopes to develop the co-operative further and is getting help and advice to diversify the income of the campesinos through pig rearing and bee keeping.

This work of the sisters isn't done without difficulties. The main one

must be the opposition of the townspeople who do not like to see anyone trying to help the campesinos to better themselves. "They call us
Communists at times," Chris told me, "because of our work with the
campesinos." ·Then there are the natural difficulties encountered in
trying to visit all the communities. But the greatest difficulty is the
lonely vocation of the missionary. "You feel a stranger everywhere,"
Justin said, "we are always foreigners here and, when we go home, the
people just aren't interested and can't imagine what it's like here."

Certainly the process of trying to change the effects of centuries of
exploitation and underdevelopment meets with more setbacks than
successes. But the four sisters in Coroico have started a process, not of
giving handouts or of doing things for the people, but of organising the
people to better themselves and this is a process which slowly takes on
its own momentum. For the sisters it has become a learning too, and
not only learning from the rich values of the campesino culture but
from their deep understanding of the Gospel as well. As Justin told me:
"I am convinced that the Gospel can only be understood by the poor."

Brazilia Teimosa: Confronting the System

The one square mile peninsula just ten minutes from the centre of
Recife, the capital of the Northeast of Brazil, has been well named.
Brazilia Teimosa it is called because it was in 1960, the year Brazilia
became the country's new federal capital, that the people moved in to
squat on this piece of land. Teimosa means stubborn, and the fact that
twenty years later twenty-five thousand people are living on this one
square mile, with as yet no legal rights to their poorly constructed
wooden and brick shacks, has indeed earned them the name.

Living with these people for the past six years has been an Irish nun,
Sr Mary Kearney. By now, she says, "I don't consider myself an outsider." Neither do the people — not because she has done things for
them (that she refuses to do) but because she has energetically committed herself to struggling with them for their rights.

The Council of Dwellers was first set up by a priest thirteen years
ago to get the people to think about their problems and act on them.
A nine-person council was elected by the people themselves with two
representatives elected for each street who act as a go-between with the
council. But for eight years it fell into the hands of the people who, as
Mary puts it, "had a different vision, they were committed to the
government and sought to do what the authorities wanted." When Mary
first began to live in Brazilia Teimosa, she saw that the council was
acting against the interests of the people, and that it was likely that the
government were going to move them out.

A group of local people who wanted a more active council responding to the needs of the people put up their candidate for the next election and after intense canvassing won the election. Then they began "reorganising the council so that it was on the side of the people seeking their betterment."

The results were impressive. They set up a commission to investigate who owned the area as the government has always denied ownership. They found, through research and the help of a lawyer from the diocesan Justice and Peace Commission, that the government had in fact owned the land after buying it from the navy in 1935, and that a consortium of businessmen was interested in buying it from them to develop it as an exclusive yacht club.

They also found that the government had a plan to develop the area, but not in the interests of the people living there. The government plan was to build exclusive restaurants and plant a wood, so presumably the people would be moved. The council therefore set up a planning commission which decided to find out what the people wanted. So they organised meetings with the people and brought their wishes to their own meeting every Wednesday night for serious study with a lawyer. In saying this, though, Mary emphasises that the lawyer only gave advice, adding "here in Brazil the people's voice is as important as the lawyer's voice."

A list of six basic demands were then drawn up by the council. These were:

1 The legalisation of all the lands in the names of the present occupiers.
2 A commitment that no one be moved out.
3 Special attention to be given to the seafront area where the houses were the flimsiest, and were often knocked down by high tides.
4 A system of running water for the area.
5 Special bye-laws to avoid the incursion of speculators.
6 The recognition of the council as the competent authority to deal on behalf of the people.

When I visited Brazilia Teimosa, Mary was taking around this list of demands to get the people's signatures. "So it is a huge success, and the people are completely on our side," she told me.

The council does not wait for the government to accede to the demands. They are actively making the people aware of the importance of getting a legal title to their land and house. This they do by holding a meeting in each of the forty-nine streets of the area. But before the meeting they send around a leaflet to each house dealing with the topic to be discussed. This leaflet is in the form of simple cartoon drawings of a character they invented called Teimosinho, little Teimosa, drawn by an artist in the city who supports their cause. The leaflet gets the people thinking about the issue.

Next comes the street theatre which does a show on every street to which all the people on the street are invited. Again they take up the same issue, just touching on the problems but not touching on a resolution. "Usually it finishes with a question: 'What shall we do, how can we do it', because the people are capable of making their own decisions, we can't do it for them," Mary says.

Before coming to the meeting, therefore, the people will have discussed the issue; and at the meeting they will have opinions to contribute. "These meetings are non-directive, just listening to the opinions of the people," Mary says. This process goes on continuously, she adds: "As soon as we finish on the legalisation of lands, we start on the need for water."

Another service the council provide is one of juridical help. A lawyer comes for two hours a week, and people with work problems or housing problems go to talk to him. Each week he sees from eight to twelve people, and provides the poor person with an access to justice which they could not otherwise afford. The council also runs a health group, since malnutrition due to the bad diet is one of the major problems of Brazilia Teimosa. Again they meet with the people, offering advice on how to make their meagre income satisfy basic nutritional needs.

The extensive work going on in the area has its impact on the wider world of Recife. Mary told me of a human rights night organised in the city to which eighty people went from Brazilia Teimosa. "We dramatised our situation for all the people of Recife so they would understand our situation, identify with it and try to organise themselves to the point of being able to stand up for themselves."

Life is a constant battle with new issues arising demanding action. Just before I visited the area, a government announcement that they intended paving the main street which the bus used caused immediate action. "We saw that in paving the street fifty-seven houses would be disappropriated with very little compensation, so we decided something should be done," Mary told me. "First of all we called the people involved to a meeting, and then we denounced the plan to the newspapers. The government were annoyed, so we invited them to a meeting here in the area, which is something new, the first time that government officials sat at the same table with the people."

The council had two main demands to put before the officials: "Because the priority is the people, we wanted a system of drainage first, before the street," and "recognising that the main interest behind a tarred street is the bus company and a yacht club . . . before anything else we wanted the legalisation of the land, because otherwise they could be paving the street with the idea of removing us someday." Seeing that the people were united behind these demands, the officials had no option but to agree.

Mary had first begun her work with church groups but soon came to the conclusion that she would prefer to work outside church structures, "because very few go to church and most of the active organisers are not church goers." But she sees her role as being very Christian: "Our motivation in all this is that, as Christians, the first thing we believe in is brotherhood, and we believe that Christ's first choice was for the poor, for the most marginalised. So our choice too is for the poor who here in Brazil happen to be the people who have very little access to justice, who are exploited, who still live in slavery. So we believe that in liberating the people to become people, to become capable of thinking, we are evangelising the people."

This constant regard for the people means that Mary refuses to give hand-outs because "we find that in putting a band-aid we are doing nothing to cure the root." In its place is the much slower but more sure task of conscientisation: "Once a man learns to understand a system, learns to see that he is a human being, that his rights should be equal to other people's rights, only then is he becoming a person, a son of God."

As a mark of her identification with the people, Mary does not earn much more than a local person earns if they are lucky enough to have work. "I teach six classes of English a week in the city earning 2,600 cruzeiros a month; a man with a family earns 1,800, the minimum salary, so I'm well off. But it doesn't afford luxury: meat is beyond the reach of the people so meat is beyond our reach too." Any money she gets from friends in Ireland or the US, where she worked for some years, goes to the council.

Though Mary, with her bright blonde hair, could never be mistaken for a local, in every other way she is one of their own. As she took me around Brazilia Teimosa, everybody knew her; after all she is the only outsider who has come to live among them. Maybe the greatest tribute came from a priest who told me after we had dropped her home one night, "Mary must be the only outsider, particularly being an attractive young woman, who could walk around here at any time of the day or night, and be completely safe."

Chapter Seven

BISHOPS:
SUFFERING WITH THOSE WHO SUFFER

"Remember the word that I said to you, 'A servant is not greater than his master.' If they persecuted me, they will persecute you."
John 15:20

"A bishop, together with the whole Church, cannot in silence watch the wide-spread violence used against the people, cutting lives short
— through malnutrition and appaling health or sanitary conditions,
— through accidents at work and on the roads,
— through excessive work hours, fatigue and impoverishment,
— through lack of jobs and
— through wages that do not cover even basic necessities,
— through lack of housing and grossly inadequate public transport,
— through fear and the stifling of the rights of association, information and trade union activities."
Cardinal Paulo Evaristo Arns, Archbishop of Sao Paulo

If leaders rarely inspire radical change, they can take seriously the aspiration of those who seek change, and so be changed themselves. This is what has happened to many bishops in Latin America. As Bishop Proaño has put it: "It is the poor who taught me the gospel."

Becoming critical of the system which causes and perpetuates poverty has also meant becoming critical of the traditional role of the church in supporting that system. As the bishops say in their Message to the Peoples of Latin America at Puebla: "We want not only to help others to self-conversion but also to be converted along with them, so that our dioceses, parishes, institutions, communities, and religious congregations will provide an incentive for living the Gospel rather than being an obstacle to it."

This chapter looks at four bishops and the different ways in which they provide prophetic leadership, how they have suffered and how they have been changed: Bishop Proaño of Riobamba; Mons. Quinn, apostolic administrator of Sicuani; Bishop Mendez Arceo of Cuernavaca, and Archbishop Helder Camara of Recife.

85

Leonidas Proaño: Being Subversive

The city of Riobamba is one hundred and fifteen miles south of Quito, the capital of Ecuador, and is overlooked by the extinct volcano of Chimborazo, at twenty-two thousand feet the highest peak in the country, and featured on its coat of arms. But Riobamba has gone down in the recent history of Latin America for a more significant reason. At 5.15 on the afternoon of 12th August, 1976, a group of forty heavily armed police burst in on a pastoral meeting in the house of the bishop, Leonidas Proaño, on the outskirts of the city. All the seventeen bishops, twenty-two priests, five sisters and twelve lay people were arrested, and driven to Quito where they were detained in prison for twenty-seven hours. The government accused the participants of dealing "with themes of a subversive character for Ecuador and representing a subversive organisation linked to other countries." All the foreigners at the meeting, (fifteen of the seventeen bishops were foreign) were expelled from the country, and it was feared that Bishop Proaño himself would also be expelled but for the enormous national and international reaction to the incident. The following Saturday at a meeting of solidarity in the centre of Riobamba organised for the return of Bishop Proaño to the city, he triumphantly declared: "The government confiscated all the documents of our meeting, but they overlooked the most subversive of all: the Bible".

The seventy year old Leonidas Proaño became bishop of this predominantly rural diocese in 1954. He boasts of the fact that his family was poor — his father was a panama hat maker — and his ministry has been characterised by his courageous defence of the poor. For him the most important thing is to "start from the recognition of the reality, in this we take account of how people are treated, with regard to their salaries, with regard to their work. This way we recognise concretely what are the mechanisms of exploitation and of oppression which are in operation, both in the city and in the country."

He goes on to elaborate what Christian faith demands in this situation: "Because Christ became man and this means, according to St. Paul that he assumed all our miseries in order to save us from them . . . we think that it is within this situation we must announce the gospel. I believe the gospel makes the authentic revolution, it is subversive. Christ came to save us from evil, and evil must be destroyed so that the Kingdom of God can be constructed."

In putting this perspective into practice, the diocese has "elaborated pastoral plans and discovered progressively transforming activity" as the introduction to their Pastoral Plan puts it. The aim of this activity is summed up as:

"1 Liberation of the concrete person from social domination and economic exploitation;

2 Liberation from the ignorance which impedes people from understanding and transforming the world, from recognising themselves as persons, from participating in society and from knowing the true God;

3 Liberation from misery and insecurity and

4 The building of the church as a community committed to this liberation."

The centre of all this activity is the Hogar Santa Crux, the large house the bishop built in 1968 outside the city which can house fifty people and in which Bishop Proaño lives with a community of nine others, a sister, a priest, two married couples and three women workers. Together the community run the house as a centre of conscientising activity both for the people of the diocese and for groups and individuals from all over Ecuador and beyond. An example of this is provided by the regular sessions for training peasant leaders. A young Colombian who was staying at the Hogar at the same time I was there sat in on one of these groups. He was amazed at the poor people's perceptiveness of their own exploitation and its causes in the capitalist system. Leaders of the diocese's basic communities come to Santa Cruz regularly for evaluations of their work, as does the diocesan team responsible for pastoral planning.

From the Hogar conscientising teams go out around the countryside to different communities, living with them for some weeks and helping to deepen their awareness of the mechanisms of their exploitation and to strengthen their unity together. Every Sunday Bishop Proaño visits a different community for the day.

In the small city are over twenty-five Christian Assemblies, groups who meet in each others' houses to study different themes. During my stay, I attended a meeting of all these assemblies together in a city-centre hall. Bishop Proaño held a dialogue with the people in the packed hall, asking them what they thought of the church, of society, and even of himself, after the studies of the Puebla documents which they had undertaken for the previous six weeks. After an hour and a half of lively discussion he suddenly asked "Would you like to celebrate the Eucharist?" Standing behind a table, dressed in his poncho, he began a simple and expressive Eucharist during which he said that it is the poor who have a faith in God and value others whereas the rich put their faith in money and exploit the poor. "Jesus came to bring division in order to restore all things to God in the Kingdom of equality," he said.

During the same week occurred the annual procession in honour of the city's patron saint organised by the main business and commercial interests in the presence of large numbers of police and military, many in battle dress carrying machine guns. It is the only time in the year

Bishop Proaño bows to pressure and attends an event organised by the rich. The following day he said he had "felt like a prisoner," and he gave an. analysis of what was happening. "The economic and political powers are seeking a unity with the religious powers," he said "in order to defend the system of sin which prevails." The army, by their strong presence "are preventing the people from knowing the true Christ who is Christ the Liberator."

But this is his "annual day of penance"; it is with the poor that Bishop Proaño spends most of his time. Every Saturday morning he leaves free for people to come to see him, because Saturday is market day when the poor come to buy and sell. I myself saw the queue of poor people waiting outside his office in the city centre. Regularly also poor people arrived up to the house to consult him.

In relating to the poor, the bishop's main preoccupation is uniting the people to attack their own oppression. He is very critical of the evangelical missionaries, financed by United States money, who go into rural communities selling a religion which acts as opium to the people and thus dividing the community. Every group which comes to the Hogar Santa Cruz comes to uncover the reality of their own oppression.

I sat in on a group of forty young people from the southern city of Machala aged between fourteen and twenty. Bishop Proaño asked them to discuss the causes of the alienation of youth in their city. From their own discussion they concluded that, for example, they "are saturated with bourgeois complexes such as fashions, music and football idols, and individualism, all of which have their roots in the capitalist system of exploitation." Their education does not help them in any way because it is "all theory, it doesn't take up real problems or give the ability to analyse the situation," they said. The afternoon the bishop spent with them, he asked them whether Christ related to groups like the Pharisees, the rich and the authorities in the same way as he related to the poor, the sick or women. The option of the Christian is to confront the system and those who benefit from it just as Christ did, he concluded.

His insistence on confronting the system is one of Bishop Proaño's characteristics. He told me of a meeting he had with some Belgian bishops at which they asked him what they could do to help him. His answer was that they should confront the system in Belgium which causes so much exploitation of the poor in Ecuador. But that was what they did not want to hear, he said, the call to conversion. The call of the Christian today is to "be revolutionary", he told me, and, if you are, "the bishops will call you a Marxist." He admitted it is much more difficult for Christians in the developed world to confront the system because the Church there is "committed to the system."

This advice does not come lightly from Leonidas Proaño. He has suffered and been obstructed for his work. Not only has he won the constant hostility of the government but also that of most of the bishops of Ecuador. But, as an American priest working in his diocese told me, "he has the people with him, which none of the other bishops have, and that is a lot more important."

Albano Quinn: Accompanying his People

The Southern Andes of Peru is the roof of the world. The trip between its two main cities, Cusco and Puno, is around three hundred miles and takes ten hours during the dry season on the dusty, pot-holed roads at twelve thousand five hundred feet. This area was the centre of the Inca empire, whoch flourished from the late 1200's until conquered by the Spaniards in 1532, and it was undoubtedly the most advanced and organised native civilisation of the Americas. Yet the descendants of these Indians today live in virtual slavery ekeing out at best a subsistence living.

The five bishops of the area have committed themselves to support-ing the struggles of the Indian people for a new society. In a Pastoral Letter, issued in September, 1978, called *Accompanying our People,* they expressed this commitment: "Accompanying our people in their difficult search for justice, and confronted by the situation of anguish and extreme misery in which the grand majority find themselves today, we the bishops with our pastoral agents feel ourselves a part of the people who by their words and actions express their protest at the established injustice and their hope for a radical change."

The letter is divided into five parts. The first details the situation the people live in, and uses quotations from local people themselves as well as from documents of the Brazilian hierarchy and *Populorum Progressio* of Pope Paul VI. "We have little and bad land," one peasant says, and the bishops provide the figures to prove it. In the area, 81% of the farms occupy less than 5% of the agricultural land while 0.24% occupy 62% of the good land. So 88% of the peasant population farm only 5% of the productive land. "We are living badly," another says, and the letter adds the fact that the peasant population consume only half the nutrients necessary for a healthy life. The ratio of doctors per ten thousand people goes from 1.6 in Cusco to 0.4 in some areas. "All the teaching is with books from other situations," yet another says; and the bishops provide the statistic that 56% of the people in the area are illiterate, and that in parts it jumps to 75%.

The conclusion is: "We are like this because its suits capitalism and the large companies" and again the bishops fill in the facts: "Those above us, the powerful, own our sources of wealth: mines, oil, land . . .

they export these products, while the majority are undernourished. They are in league with powerful international interests (International Monetary Fund, the World Bank) and they allow foreigners to work the mines and the oil and export our riches. Our Government submits themselves to their economic decisions (buying armaments and other products not in their interest) and to their political decisions (not allowing strikes in order not to diminish their profits)."

Part two of the letter is called "The Response of the People," and details how "the people have always struggled against oppression." The third part goes into what "we as Christians think of this situation." This is a series of scriptural quotations showing how the oppressed Jewish people discovered God in their struggle for liberation. It goes on to show that Jesus announced the Kingdom of justice, peace and love. "The fruit of Jesus' resurrection," it says, "is the confirmation that our God is a God of the poor, their defender, and is the security that the people, through their struggles, will come to realise their aspirations of justice and equality, eliminating the sin of the world, because Jesus struggles with them."

The fourth part is a denunciation and condemnation of this situation. It lists specific causes of complaint by the people, rising cost of living, excessive taxes, unjust distribution of land, lack of medical attention, repression, the indifference of the government, the manipulation of the media, the inhuman conditions laid down by the IMF, in short "the economic, social and political system which ignores the interests of the majority while benefitting the few."

The final section is called "The Duties of the Southern Andean Church." Here the bishops say: "Because the gospel is understood clearly and directly by the people we commit ourselves to revise continuously our action, attitudes and life style according to the option we have made for the poor."

Monsignor Albano Quinn, the Canadian-born prelate of Sicuani, one of the area's five dioceses, allows this option dominate his pastoral action. The aim of his work is to help the people become independent, he says. One way of doing this is through bible courses which he emphasises are a means to help the people recognise the reality of their situation. Another is through the *equipos,* teams made up of a lawyer, a nurse, a vet and an agriculturalist, who travel around trying to help the people improve themselves. Mons. Quinn emphasises that not all these are Christians, but they are people impressed by the work of the diocese who want to help it advance. When I visited them they were planning to set up a Justice and Peace office to further the work for change. Mons. Quinn sees the need for trained lay leaders who are not just leaders in church affairs, but who are community leaders too, and whom the church could support in their activity. As an extension of this he does not want to train what he calls "career priests", but to provide a setting to give men a training for the priesthood that will still allow them to go back to their communities to help at harvest time and whenever they might be needed. He hopes to set up an experimental training centre soon.

A further expression of the diocese's work for change is their support for strikes. They have allowed strikers to meet in churches, and have supplied them with food and drink. They were discussing whether to support a forthcoming teachers strike when I was there.

Mons. Quinn is a tall, powerful man, but is affectionately called "tiny" by all who work with him. With Peru now moving from military dictatorship towards parliamentary democracy, Mons. Quinn believes the task is to find where the church as church finds into this process. He is very critical of those who rest easy with their traditional faith which says nothing to the reality of the people's lives. "Christians," he says, "must get involved in politics. It may be harder, but we must work for radical reform of society."

Sergio Mendez Arceo: Supporting Socialism

The day I met Bishop Sergio Mendez Arceo of Cuernavaca in Mexico, he was attacked by a fellow bishop on the front page of one of Mexico's leading dailies for supporting guerilla violence. This is nothing new for Bishop Mendez Arceo, who in 1977 celebrated his twenty-fifth anniversary as bishop. In February, 1978, he was the centre of a national controversy. In an open letter which he together with the Nicaraguan priest Ernesto Cardenal and a Christian who is a member of the Central Committee of the Spanish Communist Party, wrote in Cuba that month, he said that "the socialist revolutions which have been carried out all over the world constitute the great challenge which today is presented to the church. In Latin America this challenge is decisive: according to the response of Christians, the revolutionary process will follow one course or another and at the same time the action of the Church in history will fulfill or not the call which Jesus of Nazareth has given it."

The Mexican daily *Excelsior* falsely reported the bishop as saying that the Kingdom of God cannot be brought about without resorting to Marxist thought. The presidency of the Mexican hierarchy therefore, without consulting Bishop Arceo or checking whether in fact he had said this, issued a statement affirming that "there are systems, such as Marxism, which have a vision of the human being, of history and of society which is incompatible with the Christian faith."

The statement of the bishops caused immediate reactions. The priests of the Cuernavaca diocese issued a public letter saying: "We are witnesses to the risk and decisive option our bishop has taken for the poor and the oppressed as a result of his following Christ. . . . The way he has been attacked leads us to suspect that behind the behaviour of the bishops' presidency there are other interests than those distinctively pastoral." A group of sixteen Brazilian bishops wrote a public letter expressing their "surprise and displeasure because of the way you were publicly judged and condemned without previous dialogue and without the possibility of public defence on the accusation of an alleged doctrinal offence based on a single distorted quotation by the press." They went on: "We know your passionate fidelity to the Lord Jesus, to the church — a church which we, like you, want to be poor and committed to the Kingdom — and to the oppressed people of our America. We also want our gesture to be one more affirmation of the pluralism of options with which the Church of God lives in the world of men in the fellowship of one faith."

Yet, for a progressive, Bishop Mendez Arceo comes from an unlikely background. A seminary professor with a doctorate in history, he was renowned for his firm authoritarianism when a teacher. One writer, on the occasion of his twenty-fifth anniversary, spoke of him as "a fantastic example of personal change, some say of conversion." A priest who studied under him and who works in his diocese, Rogelio Orozco, sees three stages in his life as a bishop. The first was "as a superior, who comes to govern and who wishes that all runs smoothly." After that came a stage "in which he held more dialogue and he wanted to win the confidence of his priests." Finally, he arrived at the stage "where he gives entire freedom to each one to go his own way searching for the common good of the church in dialogue with his comrades in the area he lives."

As a bishop he seems to have always been a man ahead of his time. In 1957 he began the renovation of his cathedral and introduced liturgical reforms anticipating Vatican II. In trying to create a living liturgy with the active participation of the people, he began to proclaim the readings in Spanish. This led him to realise the need people had to study scripture. So he started a biblical movement in his diocese with hundreds of small groups and families reading and discussing the Bible together. By September, 1962, Cuernavaca had ten thousand Bibles and thirty thousand New Testaments. From this grew ecumenical relations, based on biblical discussion. In that same year, Cuernavaca held a Biblical Congress, an official Catholic function with Protestant participation.

It was in this period too that Cuernavaca attracted Ivan Illich who set up his famour CIDOC language and acculturation centre. This centre brought some leading theologians to the city, and around these Don Sergio organised monthly days of renewal for his priests to enable them to analyse together their pastoral experience.

Don Sergio also encouraged the growth of CEBs, though his style is not so much to take a personal hand as to allow those involved to do what they think is best, and from time to time to discuss with them what is going on. "He will never stop anything going on," a pastoral worker in the diocese told me, and gave the example of the charismatic movement which has come to Cuernavaca by way of the many Americans living there. While the bishop regards it as "a spiritualistic movement of refuge" and refused to give his blessing to it when asked by one of his priests who was involved, he would not stop it being established in the diocese.

Meanwhile Don Sergio himself has been becoming more and more politicised. As one priest friend of his said: "From his contact with reality and from study, his definitive criticisms against capitalism and the private ownership of the means of production were born." In 1970 he said that "only socialism can bring true development to Latin America" and that socialism is "more in conformity with the Christian principles of fraternity, justice and peace," and added, "for my part I believe one ought to be a democratic socialist." This commitment he has put into action by being the only bishop at the founding meeting of Christians for Socialism in Chile in April, 1972 and its follow-up in Ottawa in 1975.

In 1975, also, he participated in the Tribunal in Mexico which condemned the crimes of the Chilean military junta and, in 1976, in the Tribunal in Greece organised by the World Council of Peace to condemn the violation of human rights in Chile. In August 1978 he was the only foreign churchman invited by the Cuban government to participate in the Eleventh World Festival of Youth and Students in Havana. Probably the most moving witness to his commitment to socialism was the sad pealing of the bells of his cathedral at 7.00 p.m. on 11th September, 1973 in mourning for the death of Salvador Allende.

When I spoke with him, Don Sergio spent most of the time clarifying his views on socialism. We need, he said, "to talk not just of socialism, but of Marxism. Naturally we don't use Marxist philosophy, but Marxism in as much as it is an analysis of society, and also as historical materialism, an analysis of history." It also leads us "to a profound reflection on our faith. A political solution is necessary to our problems," he added, "so as all can share in the goods of the earth. The modern world cannot be transformed without Marxist discourse, and this discourse is a culture, a mode of thinking, of speaking. For example, we all talk now about the class struggle, or about alienation, that is part of Marxist discourse." He then spoke about the controversy he had been involved in: "It was attributed to me that I said that the Kingdom of God can't be brought about without Marxism. What I said was totally different. I said that the modern world can't be transformed without taking Marxist discourse into account. But, of course, there are links between Christ's Kingdom and transforming the modern world. We cannot absolutise socialism — it is a creation of man for the advancement of man. My faith in the Lord, on the other hand, is absolute."

Don Sergio, who has visited Cuba many times, went on to say that "it is precisely because of experiences in Cuba that we can talk about strategic alliances between Marxists and Christians. What for? So that the goods of the world can be distributed to all, and so that all are clothed, have food, have living quarters, have medicine, etc., etc. Cuba is different from all other Latin American countries in that it is quite obvious there, in Santiago de Cuba, in Havana, or in their other cities, that they don't have zones of misery as do most of the other principal cities of Latin America."

The bishop turned then to the fear many have of Marxism. "If the poor are afraid of Marxism, it is because it has been injected into them by the powerful and by the media of communication. Naturally in an industrialised, abundant, consumer society as is the US there are fears which the political capitalist system plays on to perpetuate. The Church of Christ must be poor and be among the poor. The proclamation of the Gospel to the poor is a privilege; the rich can't hear it without being converted and they deny it because of the other transitory cares they have."

Don Sergio Mendez Arceo has not been willing to sacrifice the call of the Gospel to easy popularity or to his status as a church leader. In the words of a man who has worked closely with him for the past eight years, "he is probably the most progressive bishop in the world."

Helder Camara: Inspiring Change

Though Archbishop Helder Camara of Recife, Brazil, must be Latin America's best known progressive bishop, and although he has spoken throughout the world of the need for radical social change, he professes that as a young man he was a staunch conservative. "The seminary," he says, "was unable to give me any wide or firmly based social vision. On the contrary, I left there seeing communism as the evil of the century, the evil of evils itself. To accept and defend the established order and authority seemed to be my duty as a man and a Christian."[1]

After his ordination in 1931 Dom Helder worked to advance the Integralist Party, a right-wing movement influenced by fascism in Europe. At the young age of twenty-six he became Director of the Department of Education in his home state of Ceara in the Northeast. In 1936 he was invited to work in the Federal Ministry of Education in Rio de Janeiro by Cardinal Leme but by this time he was already becoming critical of fascism under the influence of the writings of the French Catholic philosopher Jacques Maritain.

Six years later he began to work in religious education in Rio, and branched out into the Catholic Action movement which took him all over the country learning about the place of the church in Brazilian life; or, as he puts it himself more often, its "non-place." This work also brought him to the notice of the Papal Nuncio whom he told of the need to set up a national organisation of the bishops with its own secretariat. So this was the proposal that he took to the Vatican Secretary of State, Monsignor Montini (later to become Pope Paul VI) when he made his first visit to Rome in 1950. When the CNBB (the National Conference of Brazilian Bishops) was created in 1952, Dom Helder was appointed as its first Secretary General, a post he held until 1964.

In this job, he was the main organiser of both the International Eucharistic Congress in Rio in 1952 and the first General Conference of Latin American bishops, (the predecessor to Medellin and Puebla) also in Rio in 1955. It was at this latter meeting that CELAM, the permanent organisation of Latin American bishops, was set up and Dom Helder served as its vice-president for three terms. He claims that it was a remark by Cardinal Gerlier of Lyons, who congratulated

him on his organisational abilities, and asked him why he did not put these to use in solving the problem of the slums of Rio, which began his next phase of work.

He planned a project to rehouse some of the slum dwellers in blocks of flats, using the resources he had gathered to organise the two major conferences. In three years he had managed to rehouse about a thousand families in newly built areas. But, looking back on it now, he says: "It didn't go to the root. It only called attention to the problem."[2]

As General Secretary of the CNBB he had also organised delegations of the bishops to meet the President of Brazil to discuss the urgent social problems of the country and demand immediate action. He was becoming particularly aware of these problems through being national chaplain of the Catholic Action movement, and was responsible for beginning the national literacy campaign in 1961, through which Paulo Freire was to develop his ideas.

It was in this period that he was beginning to discover that "partial or local solutions were not the answer but a world awareness of the basic reason for the world's problems."[3] It was because of his increasing deununciation of capitalist society that Cardinal Jaime Camara of Rio, whose auxiliary bishop he had been since 1955, decided they would have to part company. And so, when Recife became vacant in 1964, Dom Helder returned to his beloved northeast as bishop of its principal city.

Already he was being called "the red archbishop" and since 1964 was also the year of the military coup, the distinctive mark of his ministry was clear from the beginning: "I had to have the courage to speak out as Archbishop of Recife on the importance of freedom, of justice and of truth in that decisive hour."[4] Dom Helder has not stopped speaking out since.

At the age of seventy-one Helder Camara displays what can only be called an infectious vivaciousness. He is forceful and engaging to speak to: forceful about the strong beliefs and opinions that have come to be associated with him. He refuses to believe that violence is any ultimate answer: change will only come when the people are aware and mobilised. He refuses to change his high regard for youth: maybe some sectors have become more conservative, he admits, but his strong hope is still in the natural radicalness and restlessness of youth. And, above all, his belief is in the poor and in their struggles for a radically new society.

If there is any one person in the Latin American church to whom can be attributed the inspiration for the changes that have no transformed it in the past fifteen years, then that man is Archbishop Helder Camara. His name is already a legend, his person a symbol of the prophetic church.

Chapter Eight

PUEBLA:
ENUNCIATING THE VISION

"You are the light of the world. A city built on a hill cannot be hid. Nor do men light a lamp and put it under a bushel, but on a stand, and it gives light to all in the house. Let your light so shine before men, that they may see your good works and give glory to your Father who is in heaven."

Matthew 5:14-16

"It is necessary to call by their name injustice, the exploitation of man by man, or the exploitation of man by the state, institutions, mechanisms of systems or regimes which sometimes operate without sensitivity. It is necessary to call by name every social injustice, discrimination, violence inflicted on man against the body, against the spirit, against his conscience and against his convictions."

Pope John Paul II

Bishops' conferences rarely raise much interest, far less much excitement, outside specialised circles of church people. Puebla, therefore, is a totally new experience. Not only was the world's press there in force showing the enormous interest all over the world in the conference and its outcome, but the poor and oppressed were positively looking to their bishops for a support that would give them hope and inspiration in their struggles.

The interest being shown in Puebla was not for what it might begin, but for the vision it would enunciate. Would this be the vision of the grass roots of the continent, which had been articulated and stimulated by the Medellin conference ten years earlier, or the fearful retrenchment worked for so vigorously by conservative interests (some with active CIA backing), a narrow, comfortable view of the church and its mission whose effect would be to re-inforce the status quo?

Because Puebla is just one more milestone in a historical process, the first part of this chapter fills in the background to the conference, both in looking back on the achievements of its 1968 predecessor and looking at the conflicts and divisions evident in the preparations for Puebla. Part two gives an account of Puebla as it was happening. And the final part is an evaluation, through the eyes of Latin Americans, of the conference's conclusions.

The Legacy of Medellin

The second conference of Latin American bishops held in the Colombian city of Medellin in August and September, 1968, and opened by Pope Paul VI, has proved a more significant event than anyone at the time could realise. For Jesuit theologian Jon Sobrino, Medellin has become a "symbol of the hopes and aspirations of the continent as well as of the church." For the bishops of the northeast of Brazil it was a "promise" now being fulfilled. For the Latin American Workers' Confederation it "represented a crucial moment for the workers and all peoples of Latin America." And for the peasants of Brazil it showed "the love for us which made the good seed take root."

The importance of Medellin lies in its effort to face up to the impoverishment of the majority of Latin Americans. The final documents therefore did not rest content with generalised statements, but sought to identify the root causes of this poverty. "The principal guilt for economic dependence of our countries," they said, "rests with powers inspired by uncontrolled desire for gain, which leads to economic dictatorship and the international imperialism of money." They pledged the church to "awaken in individuals and communities a living awareness of justice, to defend the rights of the poor and oppressed and to energetically denounce the abuses and unjust consequences of the inequalities between rich and poor." Furthermore, in a significant departure from a tradition of paternalism, the bishops committed themselves to "encourage and favour the efforts of the people to create and develop their own grass-roots organisations for the redress and consolidation of their rights and the search for true justice."

Medellin, then, was a symbolic moment with the church moving from the position of being the "principal support of the social order, which was clearly a social disorder", as Helder Camara has said, to a position of a solemn commitment to be with the majority, who are the poor, oppressed and marginalised multitudes, and confronting with them the "institutionalised violence" of the establishment. "In accepting this mission in the world," Sobrino says, "the church feels itself liberated to better hear and put into practice the Word of God." Moving closer to the people has also meant moving closer to the Gospel.

Furthermore, the authority inherent in the Medellin conclusions does not derive primarily from the fact that they come from a conference of bishops, but rather rests in the clear prophetic tone of those conclusions. They served as an inspiration, and led to the commitment of countless groups and individuals all over the continent. The following testimony of an Argentinian who was at Puebla serves as an example:

At the time of Medellin, I was sixteen years old. Medellin gave to young people reasons to live, reasons to hope; above all it helped us to see that Christ had identified himself with the poor. We formed small prayer and reflection groups, and we began to see the necessity of living and working with the poor. This, for me, was a true conversion in the sense that all the plans I had for my life were called into question, when I realised how serious the needs of the poor were.

But when we began to act on our convictions, the military became suspicious of us. As a result, many of us were arrested and imprisoned. Others had to go into exile. So, when we learned that the bishops were going to meet again, in Puebla, we came here to ask for their support, to ask them to remember that we began because of what they said at Medellin. Because we are children of Medellin.

But not all were children of Medellin. Bishop Proaño has said that "a majority of local churches, of bishops and bishops' conferences have tried ways and means to subtly cancel out the value and the strength of the Medellin documents." Therefore the preparations for Puebla, which began in July, 1977, with meetings of bishops from different regions of the continent, were characterised by the struggle of some to put the clock back on Medellin. The general secretary of the permanent secretariat of the Latin American Bishops' Conference (CELAM), Archbishop Lopez Trujillo of Medellin, was one of the main figures identified with this effort and he used his position as chief organiser of Puebla to try to weigh both the preparatory document and the representation at the conference in favour of the conservative side.

The original *Documenta dè Consulta,* drawn up in 1977 and sent out to groups all over the continent for reactions, was widely criticised for its conservative approach. A group of leading Peruvian theologians said that they "experienced a deep sadness after reading the document which is dominated by fear, intellectualism and defence against danger."

Many criticised the document for its naive belief in industrialisation as a way of solving the continent's problems without taking into account the glaring inequalities in distribution of income and access to resources, or the acute dependence of Latin American economies on outside forces. As Bishop Fragoso of Crateus, Brazil, put it: "The emphasis should be on dependency, and hence on liberation, to which all Christians are called together with all oppressed people." He elaborated on the document's belief in progress through education: "It does not seem correct to me to say that the primary problem is cultural. Critical consciousness is not enough to ensure the victory of a new civilisation. Critical consciousness is not possible without organised struggle against structural forces obstructing liberty."

Neither did the document incorporate the perspectives of the theology of liberation. "Is it," asked Bishop Fragoso angrily, "that the authors or collaborators were so sectarian as to disregard the effort of theological reflection painstakingly carried out in Latin America in the last ten years?" But the effort to exclude a liberation theology perspective from Puebla went even further. The list of *periti,* official theological advisors to the bishops, which at Medellin had included the leading progressive theologians, excluded all theologians associated with liberation theology. In place of these, the organisers invited twenty theologians and social scientists, all of them conservative. Included were men like Renato Poblete from Chile, and Europeans Bonaventura Kloppenburg and Pierre Bigo, well known opponents of liberation theology. In spite of this, some bishops did invite liberation theologians to come to Puebla as their personal advisers.

So manipulative were the efforts to discredit liberation theology, that a group of leading German theologians issued a statement criticising the activities of a Belgian Jesuit, Roger Vekemans, one of Archbishop Lopez Trujillo's helpers, because he was getting financial and moral backing from German church groups and a German bishop for his work "against the self-liberation of poor and oppressed people", as the German theologians put it. Even Fr Arrupe, the Jesuit General, issued a press statement dissociating himself from the work of Vekemans.

An example of this manipulation in action was in the choice of delegates to the conference. Out of the three hundred and fifty delegates, only one hundred and seventy seven were elected by the different national episcopal conferences. The bulk of the remainder were either directly nominated by the organisers or by the Vatican after consultation with the organisers. An example of the type of delegates nominated was the layman from Guatemala, a very poor country with over 50% of its population Indian. He was J. Skinner Kell, the local representative of the US transnational corporation, Helena Rubenstein! Among the bishops nominated by the organisers were some of the most conservative of the continent. The final result was that representation was strongly weighed in favour of the conservative interests.

The response to these preparations was an enormous richness of documents drawn up by groups all over the continent expressing the hopes of the popular church for "translating into action the imperatives of liberation of the people and refusing to allow the church to be used to endorse the prevailing socio-economic systems which create the marginalisation and exploitation of oppressed people," as the bishops of Sao Paulo said. These documents came not only from bishops and theologians but also from peasant and workers' groups and from basic communities. In them are expressed the intense living faith and commitment of the post-Medellin church as well as the fear that Puebla would opt for a more traditional way. Bishop Proaño summed these up on the eve of the conference: "I strongly hope that Puebla will be a step forward, an expression of closer fidelity to the Word of God and to the cry of the Latin American people. But there are some who want to move backwards to a pyramidal church, a church without conflict, to the construction of a Christendom-type church. Thus, I believe there will be a confrontation in Puebla, and no one can predict which of the two tendencies will triumph."

Puebla, Day by Day

Puebla, a city of almost a million people, some eighty-five miles south of Mexico City, was an unlikely site for the Third General Conference of Latin American Bishops (CELAM). The first city the Spaniards founded in the New World after Mexico City, and the oldest diocese in the Americas, Puebla was until recently a quaint, old, traditional, colonial town dominated by a few rich families. The influx of industry in the last twenty years, with the huge numbers of poor who came seeking their fortune, changed the conservatism of the city very little. The rich still live in incredible luxury in huge modern mansions on the north of the city, and, within five minutes drive, you come across unpaved, unlit streets with families of ten or twelve living in huts made of cardboard. Over half the city's population live in these poor *barrios,* some of them over the years building little houses of bricks, some of them never getting beyond their corrugated iron or cardboard shacks.

The huge Palafaxiano seminary where the conference took place, lies in the outskirts of the city. A modern building, more reminiscent of a luxury hotel than a training college for priests, most of whom will have to work among the poor, its high walls and thick steel gates seemed to symbolise the efforts to exclude the reality of the people from the conference. Entry beyond those gates was strictly supervised, and was restricted to delegates and accredited press personnel only. Within, the press were restricted to two large outer halls, far from the delegates and the debates.

On Friday, 26th January, 1979, Pope John Paul II arrived in Mexico City. The following day he formally opened the conference with a Mass celebrated by himself and all the conference bishops in the Basilica of Our Lady of Guadalupe in the capital. On the Sunday the Pope travelled

by road to Puebla where he officially inaugurated the conference pro-
ceedings with a public Mass in the huge seminary grounds and a long
address to the delegates in the conference hall.

The coverage of the Pope's talks during these three days in most of
the Mexican press was distorted in the extreme. Headlines like "Anti-
communist Pope" and "Pope attacks Theology of Liberation" were
typical. However, such reporting completely overlooked his call for
"a more just and equitable distribution of goods, not only within each
nation but also in the wide world as a whole"; his insistence on an
"end to systems which allow for the exploitation of man by man and
by the state"; and his deep concern at "the sometimes massive increase
of human rights violations in all parts of society and of the world",
all made during those first three days. The specific cautions he made, on
the basis of which he was alleged to have condemned liberation theology,
were directed at extreme positions not held by any reputable theologian, and were balanced by his affirmation of the developments in the
church since Medellin when he said: "The whole church is grateful to
you for the example that you are giving, for what you are doing, and
what other local churches will perhaps do in their turn." Furthermore,
he seemed to take the distorted press coverage into account, and it is
widely believed he re-wrote the talks he gave during the last three days
of his visit. Certainly, these were almost exclusively concerned with
social and economic matters, and he even gave some political advice
telling peasants "there is no doubt about expropriating private property
if the common good demands it", and he asked workers to "take a
greater responsibility for the construction of a new world order".

The campaign against liberation theology continued, however. There
were demonstrations by young people in the city streets chanting
slogans like "Christianismo, si. Socialismo, no," and handing out leaflets
saying: "Communism is a mask: it hides hunger, misery, crime, destruction, robbery, death." One of these demonstrations called itself a
"Popular Catholic Demonstration against the Marxist Theology of
Liberation". Two different press conferences were held, one by a
group called The Movement of Fathers of Families, and the other by
the Chamber of Commerce, whose main aim was to denounce by
name cardinals, bishops, theologians and priests accusing them of
being Marxists and in "open rebellion against the pope."

Such denunciations had little effect within the conference. Despite
the greater representation of the conservatives, the delegates voted to
elect their own steering committee instead of allowing the organisers
appoint one, and, in the event, elected a mildly progressive committee
with the moderate Archbishop Marcos McGrath of Panama City as the
chairman. He thus became one of the key figures of the conference.
Moreover, the bishops also voted to choose their own themes for

discussion instead of following the inadequate preparatory document. By the middle of the first week the delegates had broken up into twenty-one different commissions, each of which would draw up a report to constitute part of the final documents. Some of the subjects chosen showed a greater openness to the Latin American reality than had been the case with the preparatory document. These included commissions on "The Dignity of Man", "Evangelisation and Human Promotion", "Evangelisation, Ideology and Politics", "Preferential Option for the Poor", and "Action with the National and International Society."

Perhaps the most significant event of the first week was the decisive pushing aside of Archbishop Lopez Trujillo in his manipulation of the conference. He had personally denied the press accreditation of five well-known church journalists, two Spanish priests, one of them writing for the official magazine of the Spanish church, *Ecclesia,* two Mexican Jesuits, and Garry MacEoin, an Irish American writer. Protests against this were supported by the whole press corps, and won the sympathy of many bishops. But the fact which shocked delegates most was the publication on the Thursday of the first week in Mexico's only progressive daily, *Uno mas Uno,* of a letter by Mons. Trujillo to a Brazilian bishop. He told the Brazilian to prepare his "bombers" and to get into training as a boxer does before the world championship so that his blows might be "evangelical and certain." He called the ideas of Leonardo Boff "confused and disagreeable;" and, even though he said he had read one of Boff's books, he kept calling him Woff. He also expressed concern at the list of supplementary delegates to Puebla, and said that the General of the Jesuits, Fr Arrupe, was invited "through the pressure of others," which he added, "leaves me with more than one doubt."

Events outside the seminary proved much more interesting, however. At press conferences organised every night in the city, the leading theologians and bishops of the continent had a forum to put their views across. Bishop Proaño of Riobamba attacked the "system of sin which in our countries is the capitalist system," and said that the church must really become poor by giving up "its riches, its privileges, and its self-sufficiency." When asked whether he thought the pope has condemned priests being involved in politics, he answered: "It is impossible to avoid politics; if we do, we must keep silent."

Gustavo Gutierrez spoke another night saying that "love for the world goes out from the position of commitment to and solidarity with the poor. If we don't start with those who are dying today, the campesinos, the workers and also the priests and religious, how can we proclaim the Christ who overcame death?" In commenting on the attacks on himself and other liberation theologians (one banner headline in an evening paper had called Fr Gutierrez "a liar"), he said, "The good thing is that we are not attacked for what we lack, but for what we have."

We heard the quiet spoken priest-poet of Nicaragua, Ernesto Cardenal, who was then International Spokesman of the Sandinista guerrillas, tell us of the need for armed struggle to free his country. He praised the support the Nicaraguan hierarchy were giving the people's struggles, and said that ultimately it did not matter what the outcome of Puebla was. "The revolution is effective love," he said, "and no episcopal document can forbid that." Later, in a city centre plaza, he showed a film about the atrocities of Somoza, and afterwards a folk group played Nicaraguan songs. Fr Cardenal has since become the Minister of Culture in the new Nicaraguan government.

Despite their official exclusion, virtually all the leading names in liberation theology were present in Puebla, some as advisers invited along by bishops. They worked quietly, preparing some forty short position papers on important issues such as "The Role of Transnational Companies", "Wages and Salaries", "The Ideology of National Security" and "Violence". These were given to bishops sympathetic to their position; and I was afterwards told that sections of some of these appear in the final documents of the conference.

Meanwhile, within the conference, trends could be discerned in the reports we were getting of the plenary debates. On one side bishops were emphasising the dangers in the new directions the church was taking. One Argentinian warned: "We may not make ourselves accomplices, by our silence, in the mutilation or destruction of the faith." The theology behind this position was summed up by a Colombian bishop who reminded the delegates that "man's vocation is to eternal bliss" and "the doctrine of everlasting life gives meaning to suffering in this world."

Opposing this point of view, and stressing the need for the church to take on the hopes and suffering of the people, a Paraguayan bishop said that the church "should be a creative force to promote and defend all authentic human values, embrace the whole of man's life, and be in solidarity with his history." In counteracting the fear of being infiltrated by ideologies foreign to the Gospel which loomed large in the minds of some bishops, auxiliary Bishop Schmitz of Lima drew applause when he pointedly advised: "Let he among you who is without ideology cast the first stone."

The report of the twenty-one commissions were revised four times on the final Sunday (11th February). Each of the drafts was voted on separately, and some, because they dealt with different topics, were voted on in three or four parts. The results of the vote showed substantial differences in the voting on each text, with large minorities against some. In the circumstances, it was surprising that only one text was voted down. This was the second part of the controversial report of Commission One on the "Social and Cultural Context of Evangelisation" which contained a strong critique of capitalism. Its revision by the conference presidency, which was finally accepted by the delegates, did not significantly change the text, however.

Puebla ended in a welter of administrative inefficiency on the night of Tuesday, February 13th, with press people having to wait until late in the night to receive even half of the final documents. Equally confused were the initial interpretations of these documents, with some claiming an advance on Medellin, and others despondent at what they saw as a consolidation of the traditional church.

Evaluating the Conclusions

The months after Puebla saw a thorough evaluation of the final documents right around the continent. It is this evaluation by the leaders of the church, many of them present at Puebla, which I present here, an evaluation from the standpoint of building a popular church.

For all, Puebla was an advance on Medellin. Archbishop McGrath of Panama City calls it "a more mature document and the sign of a more mature church." It involves, he thinks, "a serious recognition and a mature acceptance of Medellin's orientation and lines of action, and brings these to bear on the new areas that have opened up before us."

Archbishop Romero found in Puebla "sufficient elements to be used in our pastoral work. I speak especially of the denunciation of injustices and of the abuses of power, the dangers of the idolatories, as they call them, of money and materialism. There are plenty of phrases and sentences which fit in well with our priorities here. So I'm content because of the validity which Puebla gives our work."

Bishop Mendez Arceo was not elected a delegate to Puebla by the Mexican hierarchy, but he followed the conference very closely and paid a one-day visit to it. He, too, thinks Puebla is an affirmation of Medellin, "but the documents have less concentrated force. For those working for the transformation of Latin American society there are two or three documents on justice and peace which they can cite. That is good, because at Medellin you had a virginal situation, whereas now we have a situation of struggle; and every word, every phrase, has been thought about by both factions."

Bishop Enrique Alvear, auxiliary of Santiago, outlines what the core of Puebla is for him: "After outlining the catastrophic situation of social sin, the insitutionalised injustice, the permanent violation of the dignity of the person, the manipulation of the media and of education by the minority groups in power, Puebla asks what line of theological and pastoral action should we take to guide the evangelical task of transforming this situation? From this we move to the option, the commitment to action. Firstly, the preferential option for the poor: the world of the workers, of the peasants and of the poor in general. We must guide them to find the way to their liberation, because they themselves are agents of their own liberation. The second option is for youth who can be the great liberating force of society and of the church. But of all these the poor are the most important because we want a society where the poor can be persons, in which they can participate."

The most important specific aspect of Puebla for Bishop Mendez Arceo is that "the bishops have accepted that there are differences among them, though they say these are not divisions. How could we deny this, since it is more than ever visible in every meeting? Our hopes, our dreams are different: we differ because of our conditioning, studies, experiences. But, as Puebla says, we can overcome these differences so that they don't cause division."

Archbishop Romero thought that the concrete description of who the poor are is the most important element of Puebla. "Now, when the church talks of its option for the poor, it is without ambiguity: it is the face of the Indians and of the Afro-Americans who are the poorest among the poor; it is the face of the workers and the peasants who don't have the right of association. This is a concrete list and is for me a very valid step beyond Medellin. Another concrete step onwards is when it speaks of the church having to give up its privileges. Puebla has gathered these points together, elaborated on them, and made them more mature."

While the general consensus is that Puelba is a step beyond Medellin, few are entirely satisfied with it. Bishop Adriano Hypolito of Nova Iguaco, outside Rio de Janeiro, has possibly been the most outspokenly critical of the participants: "Puebla doesn't say anything new for Brazil except perhaps to affirm a position taken a long time ago. It doesn't live up to my hopes, it could have been much better. Most importantly, it lacks a prophetic gesture. For me there was no real interest among the bishops in making any prophetic gesture."

Bishop Mendez Arceo is especially critical of what Puebla has to say on ideologies: "Practically speaking, it says that a good Christian cannot hold an ideology. That people function without ideology just isn't true. The question is: what is our ideology? We must try to have an ideology which more adequately analyses the true nature of our society and world — unless we don't want to understand at all, that is. There is specifically a fear of Marxism: it is dealt with from the point of view of principles without taking into account its historical aspects. If there is a denial of it, it is because it is atheistic."

It was the Jesuit theologian Jon Sobrino, author of the much acclaimed *Christology at the Crossroads* who gave me a most comprehensive analysis of the Puebla conclusions. Going to Puebla, he said, "there wasn't much hope, I said it would be a fiasco. When I read the documents now, I see they're not that bad, though I'm not that excited about them. The people who had greater expectations and hopes will be disappointed because in general they're not strong enough and are theoretically rather poor.

"I firstly find things of importance which are missing," he told me. "The humble recognition that the church has been an important part of the problem of the continent is not there. The division within the church, which is a scandalous fact, is not clearly stated. The relation between faith and politics is missing; not the question as to whether priests and nuns can join political parties, because that is there, but the much more real problem of what are the political implications of the daily pastoral work of the church. The fourth and last thing which I miss in the documents is what we could call the 'martyrial' experience of the church: the real fact that so many people, thousands of them, even at the level of bishops, priests, nuns, catechists, have been either murdered, put in jail, threatened and so forth."

Secondly, Fr Sobrino finds tensions within the documents "between a formal theoretical framework and the contents." An example of this is the tension between "the doctrinal documents and the more pastoral ones. To put it more concretely, the documents on ecclesiology (the church) and Christology (Christ) are very poor, whereas other documents which are more directed towards the pastoral life of the church and especially the document which describes the situation in Latin America is much better." Another tension he finds is between liberation, on the one hand, and communion and participation on the other. "Both things are good, obviously, but liberation implies more the process of the church and the conflicts within this process, whereas communion tries to imply more that we are all one and the church itself is the sacrament of unity. The conclusion I'm sure will be that people who are more interested in liberation will quote what they say about liberation, and people who are more interested in peace and no conflicts and divisions in the church, will quote what they say about communion."

Finally, what is good about the documents? The first good thing Fr Sobrino comments on is that Puebla clearly affirms Medellin. "In the preparation for Puebla it was said Medellin was good, but now we are in a different situation here in Latin America ten years later, so we have to do something else. Puebla is very conscious that this is false, that the situation is worse than at Medellin, there is more poverty, more political repression. Publa stated and affirms that.

"It's also very important that both liberation and what's called 'the option for the poor ' appear all over the documents. Another important thing which I find is the use of the word 'idolatry', which appears very often. The idols mentioned are riches, power and sex, so that the problem of faith isn't posed simply against a background of simple atheism, but of an active belief in idols. The implications of this are that we say the rich and powerful have divinised wealth and power, and in this process of divination you don't have to justify anything, so private enterprise is automatically justified, and the victims which are offered to this type of god are justified. And it is the same with the regimes of National Security. So, the alternatives are not between belief in God and atheism, but belief in a God who gives life and belief in other gods who give death."

Whatever the evaluations of bishops and theologians, I found the groups of Christians I visited all over the continent avidly studying simplified versions of Puebla; and the final test was that they found in the documents an affirmation and an inspiration for their faith and struggles.

Chapter Nine

LESSONS:
A NEW CHURCH IN SEARCH OF A NEW WORLD

"He has shown strength with his arm, he has scattered the proud in the imagination of their hearts, he has put down the mighty from their thrones and exalted those of low degree; he has filled the hungry with good things, and the rich he has sent empty away."
Luke 1:51-53

"Because we believe that the re-examination and revision of the people's religious and moral behaviour should be reflected in the political and economic processes of our countries, we invite all, regardless of class, to accept and take up the cause of the poor as if they were accepting and taking up their own cause, the cause of Christ himself."
Puebla: Message to the Peoples of Latin America

As must be clear to readers by now, the Latin American church poses an enormous challenge to the church in the developed world of Europe and North America, a challenge to change incomparably greater than the challenge posed by Vatican II. And, because the changes of Vatican II have not even yet taken root in any widespread way, it is too much to hope that those posed by the example of Latin America will find widespread acceptance.

Fundamental to a change of structures is a change of attitude. This is the great challenge posed by the Latin Americans. It is primarily the challenge to be open to learning. We in the developed world have come to think of ourselves as being the dispensers of knowledge and skills, no less in the church than in secular matters. The call to conversion must begin with humility; the call to change must begin with an acknowledgement that we need to learn.

What we need to learn is nothing short of a revolution in our priorities and values as Christians. Without such a revolution, there can be no hope of the new world so urgently needed by the vast majority of the world's people if life is to mean anything at all for them. Without making this the centre of our concern, no new church can be born.

This chapter concentrates therefore on new attitudes, priorities and values. The authentic sign that these are new is that they lead to a rigorous critique of the old. Jesus could not have inaugurated his new *ecclesia* without showing up the blindness and inadequacy of the attitudes, priorities and values of the religious establishment of his day. One of the signs of the commitment of the Latin American church lies in their criticisms of us. They are concerned about the new.

The first part of the chapter highlights the importance of the changes in attitudes, priorities and values that have taken place in the Latin American church. The second part gives their view of the church in the developed world. Part three takes the case of the North of Ireland and shows how one Latin American analyses it. The final part is a short personal postscript.

A Twentieth Century Reformation

I believe it is no exaggeration to say that what has happened in the Latin American church in the past ten to fifteen years constitutes the most important and significant development in any church anywhere since the Reformation of the sixteenth century. Because, what Latin America has seen is nothing less than a revolution in the way the church looks at itself and at the world; and any revolution implies a total break with the old and a creative experimentation with completely new ideas and forms. Any attempt to understand the Latin American church within the prevailing categories and forms of the church in the developed world must fail; it is trying to put new wine into old wineskins.

A priest in Santiago said to me that he found non-Christians (and by this he meant Marxists in the main) or Christians who had drifted away from the church for some time, much more open to the Gospel than those who had continued to practice their faith. Those who had maintained an adherence to the church looked at the Gospel through the framework and categories of the traditional outdated theology they had been brought up on, a theology which hid the simple and attractive message and person of Jesus behind the heavy categories of salvation and redemption, natural and supernatural, sin and grace. On the other hand those who had none of these categories, but who had a deep commitment to the oppressed, could see the true person and message of Jesus for what it really is: a message of liberation for the oppressed and the downfall of the oppressors, an inspiration and a motivation for struggle.

This is the core discovery of the Latin American church, the revolutionary discovery that the Gospel meaning cannot be found in the formulations of doctrine but must be refound in every age as the Word of Life, as the message of the Kingdom; to discover that the old and imprisoning categories which dominated the church's self-understanding have to be broken open.

This process is described by Bishop Adriano Hypolito as "our tradition of separating the spiritual from the material, that is to say prayer, the sacraments, what were seen as a telephone line to God, from the world of politics, economics and culture. We did allow for the cultural, arts, to praise and glorify God; but as for politics or economics, no. This dichotomy, this separation between spirituality and life, must be overcome. We cannot separate the message of the Gospel from the real world of economics and politics."

The church, then, has broken out of an understanding in which it thought of itself as a religious institution fulfilling certain religious functions whose *raison d'etre* used to be expressed as 'saving souls.' Even though since Vatican II this terminology ceased to be used, the overriding self-image of the church continues to be as an institution which caters for the spiritual side of the person and exists alongside other institutions which cater for other aspects of the person: educational, political, economic, even sporting and cultural. As such it basically supports the status quo, though it may question it in certain peripheral ways on behalf of the less well-off members of society.

The *raison d'etre* of the Latin American church therefore is not simply different; it is revolutionary. In Bishop Hypolito's words: "The church is an instrument for the liberation of humanity." Thus, for the first time in centuries, the full human person has come to be of primary importance for the church.

In making the service of the human person, and not just an aspect of the person, the centre of the church's activity, the Latin American church has had to begin to take seriously unemployment, bad housing, bad health care, and all the other myriad of social problems that do damage to the person. In seeing these problems as of primary importance, the church has discovered politics in a completely new way.

Up to now in Latin America, and still in most other parts of the world, the church's interest in politics was, in Archbishop McGrath's words "simply the defence of church structures and church interests." But now, as the Latin American church becomes more genuinely interested in the liberation of the oppressed, so too does it lose its interest in safeguarding its power. "We are not a Church which wants power but which wants to serve, this is the revolution," says Bishop Hypolito.

In siding with the people the church discovers a new meaning for politics in the struggles of the people. As Archbishop Romero said of the role of the church: "It is necessary to call injustice by its name, to serve truth . . . to denounce the exploitation of man by man, discrimination, violence inflicted by man against his own people, against his spirit, against his conscience, and against his convictions . . . to promote integral liberation of man . . . to urge structural change, to accompany the people who struggle for their liberation."[1]

Politics then becomes the expression of religious commitment. Archbishop Romero, in speaking of the assassination of leaders of basic communities who, he said, "organised the people because it is a fundamental necessity for effective struggle," concluded: "Profound religion leads to political commitment."[2]

Furthermore, the process of moving closer to the people makes the church critical of itself and of its own past. This has led Latin American church leaders to openly criticise the church's complicity with the oppressors in the past and to urge a profound process of conversion of itself. "The church will only have credibility and be listened to when it enters a process of conversion of itself," says Bishop Hypolito. "This is indisputable — our first problem is how to convince the hierarchy of the church that it is so."

For this reason bishops will openly criticise one another. Bishop Hypolito was so incensed by the manipulation by Archbishop Lopez Trujillo at the Puebla conference that he openly criticised him from the pulpit of his cathedral when he returned home. So too, Latin Americans are not afraid to criticise the timidity of the church in the developed world. Archbishop Helder Camara says: "Religion, in capitalist areas, runs a very grave risk of being caught up in the system. They are courageous in broadcasting beautiful principles, but without sufficient energy to carry them through for the very reason, though perhaps an unconscious one, that they will themselves be effected by the process."[3]

Credibility can only come from authenticity which demands getting one's hands dirty. It is because the church has begun "working hand in hand with people who are believers and non-believers, Christians and also Marxists, for the welfare of the people," says Cristian Precht, that in Chile "people who before would have an attitude of reaction *vis-a-vis* the Church, or who would have been a bit mistrustful, have rediscovered that the church means it when it says that we are for man and for human promotion." He adds: "We haven't had time to get into a very intellectual discussion about Christianity and Marxism, how much and how little. It is much more sane to try to resolve your difficulties in terms of action without making a great philosophical debate out of it."

It is because the Chilean church has done this, has taken on, in Cristian Precht's term, "a commitment of life that is risky, that has difficulties" that the church "has a moral authority that really has an impact on the structures of society."

This "commitment of life that is risky" can be summed up in the word *solidarity*. It was solidarity which motivated Archbishop Romero to continue and even increase his harsh criticism of the Salvadorean ruling class though he knew only too well his life was in danger. It was solidarity that motivated Cardinal Arns to join an all-night sit-in with the leaders of the Engineering Workers Union in Sao Paulo in protest at the arrest of their leaders in April, 1980.

One of the most moving examples of solidarity by a group of Christians in the past few years in Latin America comes from Nicaragua. Here the famous priest, poet and monk, the quiet-spoken and shy Ernesto Cardenal, had a small community on the island of Solentiname, the largest island on Lake Nicaragua. Here, Ernesto and his two priest companions lived, worked and prayed with the local peasants. However, they could not cut themselves off from the struggles gaining momentum all over the country to overthrow the forty years of dictatorship of the Somoza family.

"The Gospel, above all, was teaching us that the Word of God is not simply to be heard but should be practised," says Ernesto. "And those peasants of Solentiname, those peasants who fathomed this Gospel so well, felt a solidarity with their brother and sister peasants who, in other parts of the country, were suffering persecution and terror; who were being imprisoned, tortured, murdered; whose women were being raped, whose ranches were being burned, and who were being attacked from helicopters by their own countrymen. Also, these peasants grew in solidarity with those, who for compassion towards their neighbour, were offering their lives in the Frente Sandinista [the guerrilla group which finally overthrew Somoza]. And this solidarity, to be real, means that one also must jeopardise one's security and livelihood." Soon afterwards members of the community went off, with Ernesto's blessing, to join the guerrillas, and finally Ernesto himself joined them, becoming their international spokesman, and travelling the world publicising their cause.

Ultimately it is this simple and unselfconscious heroism of Christians all over Latin America which speaks most eloquently of the new strength and vigour of the church on that continent. It is a vigour that takes those of us brought up in the tired and compromised church of the developed world by surprise: because it fits so comfortably into our societies we somehow have forgotten that Christianity makes real demands.

The future of the church lies in the Third World, and especially in Latin America. This is the view of Leonardo Boff who wants to see the European and North American church "become the allies of these changes taking place in the church on the periphery."

He continues: "I don't want to introduce tensions or polarisations between the church in the Third World and that in the developed world. The great problems of the church today aren't within the church: in a conflict between the European Church and the African or Latin American Church. It must be understood that the great problems today are of the Church as a whole confronted with a world growing even more technologised, more centralised, which is producing more and more problems of injustice and marginalisation at an international level.

"Understanding this, the internal forces of the church must be strengthened so that the Christian faith, whether in the centre or on the periphery of the world, has the same basic posture towards these problems. This must be a basic posture about humanising life, about justice, about human rights and especially about the rights of the poor.

"I believe that the European and North American church is taking account of this even more, and I think we can hope for a lot of support and understanding. I see this as something of the Spirit."

A Mirror on Ourselves

Just as one looks at the world totally differently when one takes the side of the poor, so too does one look at the church in the developed world of Europe and North America totally differently from the standpoint of the Latin American church. It is almost as if the scales fall away from one's eyes, and in one sudden dawning one can see the church in the developed world for what it truly is: tired, defensive and provincial.

Such is the opinion of Archbishop McGrath who, because both his parents were from the USA, and because he was a leading advocate of change at Vatican II, is sufficiently well acquainted with this church to make a judgement.

"In Europe," he told me, "one gets the feeling that you're dealing with a tired Christianity and you hear expressions like 'post-Christian period', which is surely not Christian, because the Lord hasn't returned yet." He senses an unwillingness to look at the weaknesses of the Church and a "somewhat provincial mentality about world problems", an inability to see the need for a new economic system with new trade relationships between the developed and the underdeveloped world. He sums it up as "a rather hang-dog approach".

Jon Sobrino, who was brought up in Spain and studied in Germany, has the impression that "the European church, in general, doesn't have a future." He said to me "I see a church which is on the defensive," and asked rhetorically: "What social significance has the church in Europe?" He went on to give me the reason why it has no significance any longer:

"The root of this, as I see it, is rather simple. Faith presupposes conversion, a change, and conversion presupposes sin. Conversion is difficult — not just difficult subjectively, that is obvious, but difficult objectively. We here in Latin America see this as so obvious that historically the process of conversion, of changing, of thinking differently, of running risks with the poor, is more visible. Then, if conversion is possible, faith is also possible. Whereas in Europe sin is more hidden and then, of course, there is the problem of secular culture."

For Cristian Precht the Church in Europe and North America is "further away from reality." He sees "such a weight of tradition that the new forms of the church have to give such a strong proof of orthodoxy that it takes much longer for them to come to fruition". He gave me examples of basic communities in Europe "which are considered by many of the hierarchy to be hostile and antagonistic; but many of them have been born like that because the church has been so clerical in its way of doing things."

He went on to ask a pertinent question, showing up the single greatest weakness in the church of the developed world: "We wonder why there aren't more struggles going on in Europe, because, after all, in Latin America we are suffering from many problems that could be handled much better in Europe and in the States. For instance, the great economic powers that are the basic cause of our problems. So we would like in that sense for the church to be able to have an impact and an influence on the ideologies and mentalities existing in Europe and the US so that we also could feel the effects of their actions."

When he goes to Europe, he says, "you don't have the feeling of strong participation, of a consciousness of being the church. I still find the hierarchy is weighty in Europe, whereas here we work hand in hand, and the hierarchy doesn't have to be giving directions all the time. Here is a young church, and there is an old church."

The Brazilian theologian now living in exile in Costa Rica, Hugo Assmann, also studied in Europe; and he holds strong views of the European Church: "It is not Eurocommunism but Eurochristianity which is the problem in Europe. There is a sort of neo-fascism in the church. The German church is almost completely fascist now. In France, whereas the bishops were calling for dialogue with Marxists a few years ago, their recent statement emphasises the dangers of this.

"The new spiritual movements like transcendental meditation, the looking to the East, and the charismatic movement are all of the same type; they are the religion of late capitalism. It is going to be much harder to be a Christian in Europe in this situation."

Latin American views of the Church in the developed world were summed up by Bishop Adriano Hypolito: "In the European church everything is organised, centralised, clericalised, there is an immense consciousness of the power of the clergy who control everything, and an immense weight of history. The church is like a museum and all this is a terrible impediment to its pastoral action."

The concerns of the European church are nowhere better expressed than in its theology; and Latin Americans have equally strong views on this. Cristian Precht finds European theology "a bore because it is very speculative, and you don't know where it fits in to helping you read the path of the Lord through the events of life, and how to discern what is happening."

For Jon Sobrino "what European theology tries to do, in the last analysis, is to help the believer not to lose his faith, for example to try to explain the incarnation in such a way that people might still be able to believe in it." He explained further, "If you read it, there are many books which are impressive because of the amount of scientific knowledge, for example, which exists in them. But if you ask the simple question: why did you write this book, as a Christian what are you trying to do in doing theology?" He shrugged his shoulders and went on "Whereas, here there is a very different answer to that question: we want to help the Church along with other people make a better world. Here it is very clear, whereas in Europe . . .?"

A Latin American looks at Northern Ireland

If there is one situation in the developed world which best illustrates this defensiveness of the church, its inability to look at its own weaknesses and to respond creatively to a situation of political instability and violence, it is the North of Ireland. Contrasting sharply with the inability of Irish Christians to even face the issue let alone find a creative response to it, is the sharp and critical analysis of a Latin American

Christian; an analysis which itself is a sign of the universal applicability of their new understanding of the Gospel.

Xavier Gorostiaga of Panama City studied in Cambridge, England, from 1970 to 1975, and at that time got to know Ireland not just through his visits but because, as he says, "my best friends in Britain were Irish."

Violence in Ireland, he thinks, is "not only an important Irish problem, it is a Christian problem". He told me, "It creates problems for the church, and, if this happens, the church has a sort of culpability in this problem. I think that in the case of Latin America it has been very useful for us to start with a sort of church analysis: 'What has been the responsibility of the church in the whole structural conflict of Latin America?' "

He went on, tracing the path many Latin American Christians felt they had to take, and drawing the lessons for Ireland: "Christiantiy has something to do with violence. Let's analyse that, let's go deeply into the historical roots of that, the functions that the church has played in Latin America, the functions that the church has played in Ireland. Have these functions been liberating functions or have these functions been repressive functions? In Latin America, without any doubt, the church was part of the functional establishment and played a functional role legalising the oppression in Latin America at least until the 1960s. In the 1960's the church made a sort of jump in history, a jump from a history of oppression to a history of being oppressed.

"I would say that the Irish church is very functional for the system that is creating the violence, because this violence in Ireland is not an accident. Of course, I am talking about more than the violence in the North of Ireland. This is an anecdote. You cannot explain that, if you isolate this phenomenon from the whole history of Ireland, as you cannot explain the problem of El Salvador if you isolate El Salvador from what is happening in Central America: the land distribution, the division of Central America, the role of the United States there and the Panama Canal."

Fr Gorostiaga recommends very much "for Christians in Ireland to follow the situation in El Salvador. I think the church in El Salvador can be a very good case to analyse how one can be a Christian in a sort of situation in which you have a structural violence."

Specifically, he said that the leadership of Archbishop Romero had been very important: "The Archbishop had a very good analysis of the causes of violence. It took him many years and a lot of suffering to find a sort of structural place for the church within a situation of violence; and it took him many, many months of discussion with theologians and social scientists. Speaking from my experiences from 1970 to '75 in Britain and Ireland, I didn't find at that time any sort of analysis. My only impression was that what the Irish church was doing, wasn't touching the problem.

"One of the problems is that I didn't see within the church a proper analysis of Irish problems, and I think this lack of analysis is what creates a sort of barrier for the church to understand the problems of the people. And now that the conflict in Ireland is so dramatic, the church, instead of analysing what the causes of this are, analysed the problem in a sort of static way: There is a lot of violence. Violence is not Christian. Therefore, the church has no role in this problem, because there is no historical analysis of what has been causing these problems."

But, from his experiences in Ireland, Fr Gorostiaga sees the problems of the Irish church as going much deeper than simply a lack of analysis of the causes of violence: "My impression of Ireland is that the church is completely outside the problems of the people. The problems of the people were going on at one level, and the church was thinking and acting at a different level, to say the least, to the people's problems."

He filled in this picture for me from what he saw himself:

"When I was attending Masses in rural Ireland, I was scandalised; I saw those poor people there, and the priest was as if he was talking about the moon. It had no connection with the real life of the people. I also spent six months among the Irish in north London. When I saw what the priests were talking about to those people, I said: 'My God, this is oppressive.' These people without security in their work, living in very poor conditions, living in a very mixed immigrant community, all these problems were never treated in the church.

"There was no pastoral work with the different groups. Then there was a sort of normal pastoral preaching that had no connection with the life of the people, a very, very conservative apporach, a mainly sexual approach to morality. My impression was that this church has very little to say to the people. In some ways, I thought, this church was a church of silence: the priest is talking every day, but saying nothing in relation to the problems of this community."

So, is the situation hopeless? Not so, says Xavier Gorostiaga. He sees "tremendous power and vitality within the popular church in Ireland. There is certainly a lot of fanaticism, a lot of opium, but also a lot of vitality within, at least in rural Ireland. But, at the moment, it is used as a tool to keep people passive because people aren't aware of what is going on."

Finally, he emphasised that "though I criticise the church very much, I also criticise Christians on the left or those who have left the Church because they are unable to analyse the religious factor in Ireland and the potentiality of religion in Ireland as a sort of changing movement. They say the church is a block to stop the future of Ireland, but I think Ireland has no future without the church, like Latin America. How can we define a new role for the church? If I were working in Ireland, that would be my interest."

Personal Postscript

It was a poor woman in a *barrio* of Cuernavaca in Mexico who said to me: "Don't forget us when you go back home." She need not have worried; no one who has seen the grinding poverty of the Third World at first hand could ever forget it. If this book has made an impact on any of its readers, it is small compared to the impact that the experience of Latin America made on me.

But the woman's request poses a deeper question, one very real to me as I travelled around Latin America. What can a privileged middle-class person living in the affluent society of the west do? Going to the Third World makes this an abiding and urgent question.

Discovering the church in Latin America poses its question also. For me it had two effects: to deepen my faith in the God of the Bible and to distance me from the church I live in. For the God of the Bible is always on the side of the oppressed in their struggle, whereas the God I was taught, the static and distant God of Greek philosophy, is found only by turning one's back on the world. The question posed was: how can one respone to God in the context of this Church? Writing this book may have temporarily eased the question, it has gone nowhere towards providing an answer.

The liberation theologians emphasise the uniqueness of their response to the Gospel. They warn against copying their response for societies whose social, economic, and political situations are very different from Latin America. But they do expect a response, a radically critical and challenging response, by Christians in the west to their societies. By and large, they do not find it.

When will Christians in the west throw off the caution and fear that makes even the most meagre change an enormous task? When will the church cease to be dominated by a professional set of clergy who are, in the main, secure in the old, and insecure with any creativity and initiative that demands change from them? When will vision and open-ness and affirmation replace condemnation and deception and oppres-sion? Do not these questions themselves come from the heart of the Gospel?

Latin American Christians have begun to discover the Gospel, because they refused to wait any longer for direction from most of their leaders, and they began to take initiatives for which they were often quickly condemned. Neither were these the timid and coy initiatives we in the West are familiar with. They were satisfied with nothing less than initiatives which sought to be adequate to the enormous problems of the oppressed. Only in their leaving the security of the tried and tested, did the Gospel come alive for them, because in it they found the motivation and resources for struggle.

It may be too much to hope that this book will lead to initiatives, but I do hope it communicates some of the urgency for such initiatives, and an inspiration from the example of a church that has taken them with boldness and courage. May it help at least some to see the church and the world through new eyes.

FURTHER READING

The following list gives some of the more easily accessible works to help the general reader gain more acquaintance with the subject. It makes no attempt to be comprehensive and only lists books available in English. Many of these books themselves contain more comprehensive bibliographies.

The best work on the historical background of Latin America is Eduardo Galeano: *Open Veins of Latin America* (New York, Monthly Review Press, 1973). A more basic but satisfactory account is given in George Pendle: *A History of Latin America* (Harmondsworth, Penguin, reprinted 1978).

A fascinating introduction to the 'flavour' of the Latin American Church in the sixties it affected a French priest who went to work in Brazil is Paul Gallet's *Freedom to Starve* (Harmondsworth, Pelican, 1972). This is complemented by the collected writings of Camilo Torres in *Revolutionary Priest*, edited by John Gerassi (Harmondsworth, Pelican, 1973), and a collection of documents mainly associated with Pope Paul VI's visit to Colombia to open the Medellin conference in 1968 published in Alain Gheerbrant ed., *The Rebel Church in Latin America* (Harmondsworth, Penguin, 1974). A book similar to the present one, based on the travels of an English Baptist minister who had spent thirteen years as a missionary in Latin America, is Derek Winter: *Hope in Captivity* (London, Epworth, 1972). Another useful work, though in a completely different vein, is the analysis of the Brazilian Church from the standpoint of political science by Thomas C. Bruneau, *The Political Transformation of the Brazilian Catholic Church* (London, CUP, 1974).

The basic book to be read on the theology of liberation is Gustavo Gutierrez: *A Theology of Liberation* (London, SCM Press, 1974). Chapter five of the present work provides a basic introduction to the other major titles on the same subject now available in English.

The Latin American bishop who is best known in the English-speaking world is Dom Helder Camara. Many of his own books have been published in English including *Church and Colonialism* (1969), *Spiral of Violence* (1971) and *The Desert is Fertile* (1974), all from Sheed and Ward, London. Studies of him include Jose de Broucker, *Dom Helder Camara: The Violence of a Peacemaker* (Maryknoll, Orbis Books, 1970) and Mary Hall, *The Impossible Dream* (Belfast, Christian Journals, 1979).

The official English translation of the Puebla documents is published under the title *Puebla* (Slough, St Paul Publications/London, CIIR,

121

1980). A useful companion is *Reflections on Puebla* (London, CIIR, 1980) with analysis of Puebla by Jon Sobrino, Francis McDonagh and Julian Filochowski as well as the text of a talk on liberation theology by Pope John Påul II. The same publishers issue regular small leaflets on various countries, including those of Latin America, which serve as short but incisive introductions to the political, economic and social situations of the various countries. They also publish illustrated translations of documents from various Churches in the Third World, including those of Latin America. (Available from Catholic Institute for International Relations, 1 Cambridge Tce., London NW1 4JL).

Finally, a most valuable source of information for the traveller on every country of the continent is *The South American Handbook,* revised every year, and published by Trade and Travel Publications, The Mendip Press, Personage Lane, Bath BA1 1EN.

NOTES

The following list of sources does not include the numerous local church documents which are used in various sections of the book. In every case I picked these up on my travels and, as far as I am aware, they are not easily available outside Latin America. Translations are all my own except in the case of those from the Puebla documents. They are taken from *Puebla*, Slough, St. Paul Publications/London, CIIR, 1980.

INTRODUCTION

1. Helder Camara, 'Spiral of Violence', (London: Sheed & Ward, 1971) p. 82.

CHAPTER ONE

1. From Victor Wolfgang von Hagen, 'The Ancient Sun Kingdoms of the Americas', (St Albans: Paladin, 1973) p. 222.
2. Jose Comblin, in 'A New Missionary Era', (Dublin: IMU, 1979) p. 60.
3. Pablo Richard, in 'The Church at the Crossroads', (Rome: IDOC, 1978) p. 114.
4. Cf Amnesty International Report 1979 (London: Amnesty, 1979) pp. 44-78.
5. Interview by Prensa Latina, published in The Irish Times, April 1st 1980.

CHAPTER TWO

1. Jose Marins, 'La Communidad eclesial de base en America Latina' in Puebla, no. 4, May 1979, p. 217.
2. Gary MacEoin, unpublished article lent to me at Puebla; pp. 4 & 5.
3. Jose Marins, op. cit., p. 229.

CHAPTER THREE

1. Paulo Freire, 'Pedagogy of the Oppressed', (Harmondsworth: Penguin, 1972) p. 23.
2. Paulo Freire, op. cit., p. 54.
3. Paulo Freire, 'A Painful Birth' in Roadrunner, no. 49, November 1973, p. 14.
4. ibid.
5. Paulo Freire, 'Education, Liberation and the Church', in Study Encounter, Vol. IX, no. 1, WCC 1973, p. 4.
6. op. cit., pp. 4 & 5.
7. Interview by Prensa Latina op. cit.

CHAPTER FOUR

1. Solidaridad, no. 71, pp. 19 & 20.
2. Caminando, no. 7, p. 6.

CHAPTER FIVE

1. Donal Dorr: "Third World Theology: Sao Paulo Conference," in *Doctrine and Life*, Vol. 30, no. 5, May 1980, Dominican Publications, Dublin.
2. Camilo Torres, 'Message to Christians', in John Gerassi, ed., 'Camilo Torres: Revolutionary Priest', (Harmondsworth: Penguin, 1973) p. 375.
3. Gustavo Gutierrez, 'A Theology of Liberation', (London: SCM Press, 1974) p. xi.
4. ibid.
5. Jose P. Miranda, 'Marx and the Bible', (London: SCM Press, 1977) p. 296.
6. Juan Luis Segundo, 'Theology for Artisans of a New Humanity', 5 vols, (New York: Orbis Books, 1973) Vol. 1, p. ix.
7. Juan Luis Segundo, 'The Liberation of Theology', (Dublin: Gill & Macmillan, 1977) p. 241.
8. Leonardo Boff, 'Jesus Christ Liberator', (London: SPCK, 1980) p. 25.
9. Gustavo Gutierrez, 'La Fuerza Historica de los Pobres', (Lima: Centro de Estudios y Publicaciones, 1978) p. xix.

10. Juan Luis Segundo, op. cit., p. 9.
11. Gustavo Gutierrez, op. cit., p. xxxi.
12. Gustavo Gutierrez, 'Revelacion y Anuncio de Dios en la Historia', in Paginas, Vol. 2, no. 1, March 1976, p. 3.
13. op. cit., p. 4.
14. Gustavo Gutierrez, 'La Fuerza Historica de los Pobres', p. xxxiii.
15. Gustavo Gutierrez, 'Revelacion y Anuncio de Dios en la Historia', p. 4.
16. Leonardo Boff, op. cit., p. xii.

CHAPTER SEVEN

1. Mary Hall, 'The Impossible Dream', (Belfast: Christian Journals Limited, 1979) p. 33.
2. op. cit., p. 57.
3. op. cit., p. 71.
4. op. cit., p. 76.

CHAPTER NINE

1. Interview by Prensa Latina, op. cit.
2. ibid.
3. Helder Camara, op. cit.

INDEX

126